AN AMBITIOUS PRIMARY SCHOOL CURRICULUM

Our titles are also available in a range of electronic formats. To order, or for details of our bulk discounts, please go to our website www.criticalpublishing.com or contact our distributor, NBN International, 10 Thornbury Road, Plymouth PL6 7PP, telephone 01752 202301 or email orders@nbninternational.com.

AN AMBITIOUS
PRIMARY SCHOOL
CURRICULUM

Jonathan Glazzard and Samuel Stones

First published in 2021 by Critical Publishing Ltd

British Library Cataloguing in Publication Data
A CIP record for this book is available from the British Library

ISBN: 978-1-913453-17-6

This book is also available in the following e-book formats:

MOBI ISBN: 978-1-913453-18-3
EPUB ISBN: 978-1-913453-19-0
Adobe e-book ISBN: 978-1-913453-20-6

Cover and text design by Out of House Limited
Project management by Newgen Publishing UK
Printed and bound in Great Britain by 4edge, Essex

Critical Publishing
3 Connaught Road
St Albans
AL3 5RX

www.criticalpublishing.com

Paper from responsible sources

✚ CONTENTS

✚ MEET THE AUTHORS

JONATHAN GLAZZARD

SAMUEL STONES

Jonathan Glazzard is Professor of Teacher Education and Head of Department for Children, Education and Communities at Edge Hill University. He is an active researcher and teacher educator as well as a qualified teacher. Jonathan taught in state primary schools for 10 years before moving into higher education. His research addresses issues of inclusion and social justice within education.

Samuel Stones is a lecturer, researcher and doctoral scholarship student at Leeds Beckett University. He is also a subject leader and pastoral leader within a secondary school. He has co-authored texts for several publishers and has written extensively on inclusion and mental health. Samuel's research explores issues of inclusion, exclusion, marginalisation, sexuality and mental health for children and young people. He is a senior examiner and experienced assessor, and holds a national training role with a large multi-academy trust.

✛ INTRODUCTION

The *Education Inspection Framework* (Ofsted, 2019a) places a greater emphasis on what children are being taught than previous editions of the framework. For many years, overall school effectiveness has been determined by educational outcomes. There has been an assumption that if outcomes were good, the quality of the curriculum and the teaching must also have been good. Sadly, this has not always been the case. In some schools there has been an emphasis on teaching to the test. The curriculum has been reduced to the aspects that have been assessed in high-stakes statutory assessment tests. In primary schools the subjects which are tested are mathematics and English. This has resulted, in some schools, in a significant proportion of curriculum time being allocated to these two subjects, thus leading to the marginalisation of the sciences, arts and humanities. The best schools have always provided children with a broad, balanced and rich curriculum. However, in some schools, including those that have achieved outstanding inspection grades, children have been taught a restricted curriculum and this can have far-reaching consequences.

Restricting the breadth of the curriculum can lead to children developing poor self-esteem, particularly those who struggle with English and mathematics but might excel in the arts or humanities. It has also resulted, in some schools, in a curriculum which is overly academic and lacking in creativity. Of course, English and mathematics can be taught creatively, but children should also have opportunities to be creative in a broader range of subjects. In some cases, students have started secondary school and have been unprepared for subject-specific teaching and learning in subjects other than English and mathematics. In other schools, lack of curriculum time for the foundation subjects and science has resulted in teachers being unable to make accurate judgements of what children know and can do because they have not assessed children's learning within the broader curriculum.

No one would dispute the fact that reading, writing and basic numeracy are vital skills which children must acquire by the time they leave primary school. In fact, if these skills are not acquired by then, young people experience significant disadvantages in secondary school. However, there is more to a curriculum than English and mathematics. The primary curriculum should lay the foundations for secondary education. It should also ignite children's interests in a broad range of subjects.

1

The primary curriculum should promote enjoyment, curiosity, motivation and a passion for learning. It should provide opportunities for children to be artists, engineers, scientists, historians, geographers, musicians, archaeologists, linguists and sports people. It should also enable children to become readers, writers, performers and mathematicians. A broad curriculum means that children can develop their talents and interests and all children can therefore experience success.

The *Education Inspection Framework* acknowledges that curriculum narrowing in primary schools is one of the unintended effects of statutory testing. A generation of young people have been denied access to a broad, balanced and rich primary curriculum due to the disproportionate emphasis given to mathematics and English. The *Education Inspection Framework* places a new emphasis on the curriculum which is both exciting and refreshing. This gives permission for schools to reclaim the curriculum, within the constraints of the national curriculum, and to reverse the trend of curriculum narrowing.

This book is a practical guide for schools and teachers. It starts by exploring what is meant by an ambitious curriculum. It addresses aspects of curriculum design and provides practical suggestions on how to develop an enquiry-based curriculum which provides children with cultural capital and is sympathetic to the context of the school. The emphasis on cultural capital is a significant new addition to the *Education Inspection Framework*. The book examines what is meant by a creative and child-centred curriculum and the ways in which the curriculum can be designed to support children's personal development, including the importance of character education. Further, it explores how to develop a language-rich curriculum. Finally, it provides school leaders with some practical suggestions to support them in the process of redesigning the primary curriculum.

✚ CHAPTER 1

AN AMBITIOUS CURRICULUM FOR THE TWENTY-FIRST CENTURY

CHAPTER OBJECTIVES

After reading this chapter you will understand:

+ the key aspects of an ambitious curriculum;

+ the importance of a twenty-first century curriculum;

+ the different approaches to curriculum design;

+ the importance of selecting high-quality texts to support curriculum planning;

+ the ways to promote equality of opportunity within the teaching of vocabulary;

+ the role of the curriculum.

INTRODUCTION

This chapter introduces the concept of an ambitious curriculum and emphasises its role in ensuring that all children are literate and numerate by the end of their primary education. It also situates this emphasis within the context of the school and its community so that all children can live as global citizens whilst respecting the views and beliefs of others. The chapter outlines the aspects of an ambitious primary curriculum in relation to social mobility, entitlement, knowledge, skills, attitudes and values. The characteristics of a twenty-first century curriculum are outlined and, in doing so, the importance of subject-specific knowledge is highlighted in relation to primary education. The chapter then discusses the advantages and disadvantages of knowledge-rich, knowledge-engaged and skills-led curriculum designs in order to support reflection on, and consideration of, approaches to curriculum redesign. The characteristics of high-quality texts are identified and the role of these texts is discussed. The importance of vocabulary and approaches to supporting children with special educational needs and those from disadvantaged backgrounds is also discussed. Finally, this chapter explores how the curriculum can be used to support and develop employability skills, and its role in relation to creativity as well as fostering children's motivation and enjoyment.

WHAT DO WE MEAN BY AN AMBITIOUS CURRICULUM?

The primary curriculum determines what children will know and can do by the time they complete this stage of their education. It is the heart of education (Ofsted, 2019b). An ambitious curriculum is one that provides all children with the knowledge, skills and dispositions that they need to thrive in the twenty-first century, irrespective of their social and cultural backgrounds, disability or other circumstances. It is a curriculum which provides children with the cultural capital that they need to be able to access opportunities in the future.

An ambitious primary curriculum is one which identifies challenging benchmarks in relation to what children need to know and should be able to do at specific stages of their education. Above all else, it should ensure that all children are literate and numerate by the end of the primary phase of education, but it should also ensure that children have opportunities for deep learning in the sciences, arts and humanities.

The primary curriculum should be relevant to the school and the community which it serves but it should be designed so that children can live as global citizens who can demonstrate independent thinking and reasoning, whilst respecting the views of others. It should provide children with a rich and varied range of social and cultural opportunities which extend beyond those which are available to them locally so that children understand that they are members of a global community. It should develop children's knowledge on a range of issues that affect contemporary society, including climate change, sustainability, conflict, and it should provide them with the technological skills that they will need during the twenty-first century. It should address issues of social justice, including race, disability, sexuality and gender inequalities. It should provide children with an understanding of the political system and its influence on the lives of people in the United Kingdom.

Key aspects of an ambitious primary curriculum are shown in Figure 1.1.

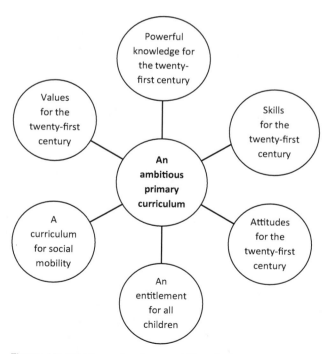

Figure 1.1 Key aspects of an ambitious primary curriculum

+ A curriculum for social mobility: the curriculum should enable individuals to access opportunities which they would not be able to access without the knowledge, skills and attitudes that the curriculum provides.

+ An entitlement for all children: all children should have the same opportunity to benefit from the curriculum, regardless of social or cultural background, disability or other circumstances.

+ Powerful knowledge: the curriculum should introduce children to subject-specific knowledge, which is correctly sequenced, so that they can take their place in society as educated citizens.

+ Skills: the curriculum should provide children with essential skills, including literacy, numeracy and technological skills. Other skills including collaboration, communication and resilience are also critical to their future success. The curriculum should also enable children to develop the skills of social and emotional regulation.

+ Attitudes: The curriculum should develop children's understanding of the importance of delayed gratification, resilience and investing effort in learning.

+ Values: the primary curriculum should provide children with inclusive values so that they can live and work within a diverse society. The curriculum should instil appropriate moral values so that children know the difference between right and wrong.

WHAT IS A TWENTY-FIRST CENTURY CURRICULUM?

A twenty-first century curriculum is one which provides children with the knowledge, skills and dispositions that they need to help them be successful within contemporary society. Children are members of a global and diverse community. Although the curriculum should be contextualised to the local community, it should also enable children to look beyond this so that they can live successful, happy and fulfilled lives.

Subject-specific knowledge is the bedrock of the curriculum. Without a secure grasp of the subject content, children will be unable to make sense of the subjects that they are learning and they will be disadvantaged. A twenty-first century primary curriculum should preserve the distinct nature of each subject. Subject-specific knowledge, concepts and skills demarcate the different subjects in the primary curriculum. These need to be clearly identified. Although there are natural connections between specific subjects, it is important that children recognise the aspects that make each subject unique. The twenty-first century curriculum should ensure that children are well-prepared for subject-specific learning by the time they reach secondary school. The marginalisation of foundation subjects in the primary curriculum has resulted in children starting secondary school without having developed a clear body of knowledge in subjects such as music, design and technology and within specific strands of science (chemistry, physics and biology). A greater emphasis on teaching separate subjects in primary schools will provide children with a firm foundation for the next stage of their education. Although thematic cross-curricular approaches to curriculum planning can provide coherence, an unintended side-effect of cross-curricular work is that subject-specific knowledge and skills are diluted or not taught in the correct order. Thematic approaches have a place in the primary curriculum but the subject is the heart of the curriculum and should not be diluted.

A curriculum for the twenty-first century must ensure that all children are literate and numerate by the time they leave primary school. If they fail to achieve these skills they will be disadvantaged and the impact of this can be long term. The primary curriculum should prioritise these skills but also ensure that children have opportunities to undertake deep learning in the arts and the humanities. In addition, children should learn the skills of emotional and social regulation and resilience through the curriculum. These skills will ensure that children can regulate their emotions and social behaviours, respond to feedback and recover from failure and other forms of adversity. These are critical skills which enable children to get the most out of their academic learning.

Learning to communicate in a different language is extremely powerful. It enables children to understand that they are members of a global community and enables them to form greater connections in the future. Learning to play a musical instrument is equally powerful because of the joy it can bring to the musician and to others. Both of these skills are extremely difficult and require a significant investment in effort, patience and resilience. Mastering these skills requires children to delay gratification but the rewards that they bring are immense when proficiency is achieved. Both of these skills are vital for the twenty-first century.

The contemporary curriculum should address current issues that the global community is facing. Examples include the effects of pollution on climate change. Children need to know how to preserve the environment

7

and the impact of pollution not only on climate but also on wildlife. The curriculum should raise children's awareness of pollution in seas, rivers, land and air and educate them about their responsibilities to the environment as global citizens. A curriculum for the twenty-first century should help children to understand how to reduce and recycle waste. A range of contemporary societal issues should be addressed through the primary curriculum, including mental health, poverty and global conflict. As members of a global community it is vital that children understand the challenges facing the global community through a well-designed and age-appropriate curriculum.

Apart from contemporary issues, the curriculum should ensure that children develop an understanding of the rich cultural heritage of the global community in which they live. They should be introduced to famous buildings, works of art, significant literature and the natural heritage, including places of outstanding natural beauty. They should learn about the lives of significant individuals who have shaped our lives, such as famous scientists, authors, poets, engineers and inventors. They should learn about famous explorers and the significance of their discoveries.

The curriculum should promote the development of inclusive values in relation to age, race, ethnicity, religion or other belief, disability, sexual orientation, gender identity and gender equality. These aspects of inclusion should be interwoven throughout the curriculum so that children can thrive within a diverse global community. The curriculum should help children to recognise that prejudice and discrimination are morally unacceptable. The curriculum should also help children to develop appropriate moral values, including knowing the difference between right and wrong.

The curriculum should promote children's awareness that investing effort in learning is worthwhile. It should also promote a range of positive character traits such as honesty, empathy, respect, courage and trust. Character is addressed in more detail in Chapter 8, in this book.

CRITICAL QUESTIONS

+ Do you agree that the curriculum should be a vehicle for social mobility?

+ Research generates new knowledge. What are the implications of this for the primary curriculum?

CASE STUDY

TEACHING ELECTRICITY

YEAR 4

Children can be taught about electricity by being given opportunities to create simple devices by constructing series circuits using components and switches. When you are teaching series circuits and switches, as well as conductors and insulators, it is important to sequence and deliver curriculum content in a way that supports children to recognise disciplinary knowledge. Therefore, children should be given opportunities to identify and understand how scientific concepts relate to each other as well as to specific disciplines within science. Teaching children about electricity provides an opportunity for discussing types of energy (electrical and thermal) and this can prepare children for learning about energy values at a later point in their learning. Children need to understand about everyday appliances that use electricity and they need to be able to distinguish between appliances that use mains electricity and battery-operated devices. Children need to understand how a circuit works and the effects of adding different components into a circuit. Throughout these sequences, making explicit reference to the different branches of science and the characteristics of each will support you to demonstrate how electricity is a physical science relating to physics rather than biology. This approach supports children to develop secure understanding of disciplines and disciplinary concepts which allows them to progress to the next stage of learning.

A possible teaching sequence for this unit of work is outlined in Figure 1.2.

Figure 1.2 Example teaching sequence

EVIDENCE-BASED PRACTICE

Research demonstrates that school inspection systems have resulted in a narrowing of the curriculum as schools have focused on teaching children aspects which are tested in high-stakes assessments (Ehren et al, 2015; Jones et al, 2017). International research demonstrates that humanities subjects have been marginalised in the primary curriculum (Barnes and Scoffham, 2017), not just in England but in the United States as well as a result of high-stakes testing (Berliner, 2011).

APPROACHES TO CURRICULUM DESIGN

Research carried out by Ofsted (2019c) identified that schools adopt different approaches to curriculum design. Ofsted categorised these approaches into three broad groups.

+ Knowledge-rich schools: These schools focus curriculum design on subject-specific knowledge that learners need to acquire. There is an emphasis on subject-specific facts and concepts that are essential to subject mastery.

+ Knowledge-engaged schools: In these schools the curriculum is designed to enable learners to acquire relevant subject knowledge which underpins the application of skills that learners also need to develop. In these schools there is no perceived tension between knowledge and skills because knowledge supports skills acquisition and skills support knowledge acquisition. An example of this is where pupils acquire knowledge of the alphabetic code (phonics) to support the skills of reading acquisition. Fluency in reading then supports children to gain knowledge.

+ Skills-led curriculum design: In these schools the curriculum is designed to support the development of critical skills such as resilience.

(Ofsted, 2019c)

CRITICAL QUESTIONS

+ Should knowledge and skills be equally balanced in the curriculum?

+ Why do children need to learn knowledge in school when knowledge is now easily accessible on the internet?

CASE STUDY

A KNOWLEDGE-RICH APPROACH TO THE TEACHING OF THE ROMAN EMPIRE

KEY STAGE 2

In a knowledge-rich curriculum it is essential that knowledge content is explicitly specified. The specifics of what children need to learn will be identified and subject-specific skills will be promoted rather than skills being taught generically outside of subject-specific knowledge domains.

In a knowledge-rich curriculum, teaching should support children to remember specific-subject content including what is meant, for example, by the terms empire, emperor, centurion and amphitheatre as well as who Julius Caesar was and where the key Roman sites are both in the United Kingdom and beyond. Children need to know about the Roman invasion of Britain and about Boudicca. The knowledge-rich curriculum will provide opportunities for children to return to Roman history throughout subsequent teaching and learning so that knowledge can be consolidated and built on in order to support retention and recall. These specific learning episodes will be identified on long-term plans and pedagogies will be carefully selected in order to support retention and retrieval.

EVIDENCE-BASED PRACTICE

The curriculum is the heart of education and subjects are the heart of the curriculum (Ofsted, 2019a). Subject knowledge for teaching includes the following.

+ Content knowledge: knowledge of the subject-specific concepts and facts.

+ Pedagogical knowledge: knowledge of effective teaching approaches.

+ Pedagogical content knowledge: knowledge of how to teach a subject.

Research has found that teachers with greater content knowledge have higher levels of pedagogical content knowledge (Baumert et al, 2010), which increases cognitive activation in pupils. This is due to the use of strategies such as effective questioning and summarising which enhance learning. However, research into the relationship between content knowledge and attainment is inconclusive. Although some studies show a positive relationship (Clotfelter et al, 2010), some show no effect (Darling-Hammond, 2000). Research has found a much stronger relationship between pedagogical content knowledge and children's progress (Baumert et al, 2010).

HIGH-QUALITY TEXTS

Many primary schools select high-quality texts and use these as a basis for curriculum planning. Schools that use this approach use the text to link different subjects, thus providing coherence to the learning that children will undertake. The selected text may last a week, half a term and some schools teach a text for a whole term. The selected text needs to be engaging and challenging. It needs to make pupils think hard. In addition, it needs to include rich and varied vocabulary so that children are introduced to a wide repertoire of language. The text should have the capacity to draw children in. It should stimulate imagination, debate, reasoning and when the teacher stops reading it, the children should be hungry to hear more.

A stimulating text can create opportunities for promoting learning in a range of subjects. Children's learning in different subjects is related to the core text and in this way a sense of overall coherence is enabled. However, the danger of this approach is that subjects can become diluted. Subject-specific knowledge, concepts and skills can become neglected or not taught in the right order and this can result in insecure subject knowledge. Systematic curriculum planning is required so that subject-specific knowledge and skills are sequenced in a logical way so that children develop a secure understanding of the subject.

High-quality texts are a fantastic way of drawing children into the curriculum. However, it is not possible or desirable to teach everything through a text. Some aspects of subject learning will need to be taught discretely because they will not fit naturally into a text or theme.

VOCABULARY

Children from disadvantaged backgrounds are more likely to have a restricted vocabulary than those from more affluent backgrounds. A restricted vocabulary limits a person's life opportunities and it impacts not only the quality of their spoken language but also the quality of their writing.

All children have an entitlement to learn a rich and varied vocabulary, regardless of social background or other circumstances. One way of addressing this is to identify the new vocabulary that children will be taught when planning units of work. Young children have an amazing capacity to learn vocabulary. Adults tend to dilute the language that they use with young children because they assume that children will not be able to comprehend more advanced vocabulary. However, if it is taught in context, children are capable of understanding advanced vocabulary and they will use it proficiently.

Children need to understand how to pronounce advanced vocabulary. It is important to spend some time practising the articulation of words so that children say the words correctly. One way of addressing this is to enunciate carefully the phonemes or syllables within words and to get the children to practise this several times. It is important to display vocabulary in lessons so that it becomes an explicit teaching focus. Many primary classrooms have lists of vocabulary on display so that children can use this as a reference point to support their writing. As children progress, they should be taught to use a thesaurus to find more interesting words to use in their writing. This improves the quality of the writing because rich and varied vocabulary has the capacity to engage the reader.

Teachers should model using advanced vocabulary in their own spoken language, particularly after specific vocabulary has been taught. In addition, correct terms should be used so that children do not have to re-learn these at a later stage. There is no reason why children should not be introduced to the correct terminology for body parts, for example.

Providing children with a rich and varied vocabulary empowers them. It enriches both their spoken and written language and it will support them in achieving social mobility in the future.

AN AMBITIOUS CURRICULUM FOR CHILDREN WITH SPECIAL EDUCATIONAL NEEDS

Children with special educational needs and disabilities (SEND) are entitled to an ambitious curriculum so that they have the same opportunities as their peers. Too often, children with SEND are placed in lower-ability groups and provided with tasks which lack challenge. This widens the ability gap between those children with and without SEND and results in underachievement. This can have a serious long-term detrimental effect. Far too many children with SEND underachieve at school and consequently are disadvantaged. As a result, many do not enter further or higher education and are denied access to employment and training opportunities.

All children have an entitlement to an ambitious curriculum which enables them to develop good subject knowledge and transferable skills. Like all children, those with SEND should be supported to develop literacy and numeracy skills. With the right kind of teaching and support, many children with SEND can learn to read, write and become numerate. Some children with complex needs may need a tailored curriculum which supports them to develop specific skills. However, teachers should always start with the mindset that children can achieve a goal rather than simply assuming that they cannot.

Providing children with SEND with a lower-level task should not be the default position. Teachers should consider ways of enabling children with SEND to access the same curriculum as their peers by building in access strategies to remove barriers to learning. Children with complex needs may require a highly personalised curriculum which focuses on the development of specific skills and some may require a sensory curriculum to enable them to learn. Children with moderate and specific learning difficulties can access the same curriculum as their peers but teachers may need to build in specific strategies to enable them to access the curriculum. Examples include the using additional adult support, breaking down curriculum content into small steps and using technology to assist learners.

AN AMBITIOUS CURRICULUM FOR DISADVANTAGED CHILDREN

Children from disadvantaged backgrounds may have less cultural capital than those from more affluent backgrounds, although this may not necessarily be the case. They may have a restricted vocabulary and they may not have had the rich experiences that financial capital provides access to. Limiting children's social and cultural experiences can impact vocabulary development, social and emotional development and the development of children's knowledge and imagination. This can affect not only children's literacy development but also their development in a range of academic subjects.

To compensate for disadvantage, the curriculum should be designed so that it is ambitious for all children. It should provide children with the cultural capital that they may have been denied as a result of their social background. The curriculum should expose children to a range of texts which capture their imagination and provide cognitive challenges. It should provide them with experiences that they have been denied, including opportunities to participate in sport, drama, dance, music, art and to learn a foreign language. The curriculum should ensure that children have opportunities to visit localities which contrast with the locality in which they live. It should promote a love of reading and poetry and ignite children's imaginations. It should provide children with opportunities to visit museums, galleries, places of worship and it should foster a connection with the landscape, including developing a sense of awe and wonder in relation to the land, oceans, lakes, rivers and the earth in space. The curriculum should promote an interest in architecture and engineering. It should provide children with knowledge of the rich social, political and cultural history of the UK and the wider world. These are all examples of ways in which the curriculum can compensate for disadvantage. There are many more examples that you will be able to think of. However, the key point is that children's futures should not be defined by their social backgrounds. Their backgrounds may limit their exposure to all these forms of cultural capital, but the curriculum can be designed to ensure that all children gain access to these so that their interests, knowledge, skills and imaginations are broadened.

THE ROLE OF TECHNOLOGY IN THE CURRICULUM

The curriculum for the twenty-first century needs to ensure that children have the knowledge, skills and attitudes that are required to be digital citizens. The pace of technological development during the last three decades has been nothing short of remarkable. Technology is now a central component of everyone's life. It is central to the modern workplace and it plays a vital role in facilitating communication and knowledge exchange across the global community. It is a key component not only in people's homes and workplaces but also in the outdoor environment. Although we cannot predict what the future will look like, we can predict with certainty that technological development will continue to advance, and that technology will play an even greater role in people's lives as we progress through the twenty-first century.

The curriculum for the twenty-first century needs to be designed to ensure that children develop digital literacy skills. This will enable them to be confident users of technology. It should ensure that they develop proficiency in a range of skills and can confidently use hardware and software, including computers and mobile devices. The curriculum should be designed so that children become proficient in the use of Web 3.0 technologies because these are already playing a significant role in people's lives. In addition, the digital curriculum should ensure that children know how to keep themselves safe online and support them in critically evaluating content that they see online. It should also ensure that children understand the importance of digital citizenship. As digital citizens children have a responsibility to treat other people with respect online. They also have a responsibility to challenge and report online abuse. Children need to understand their rights and responsibilities as digital citizens and in particular their responsibilities towards other people.

A CURRICULUM FOR FUTURE LEARNING

The primary curriculum should be designed so that it prepares children for the next stage in their education. This means ensuring that children have the required level of knowledge, understanding and skills in

16

all primary curriculum subjects so that they are well prepared for secondary education.

This means that curriculum design needs to prioritise subject-specific knowledge and skills. The curriculum should be designed so that primary school children are given opportunities to work as authors, mathematicians, historians, scientists, artists, musicians, geographers, designers and engineers. Subject-specific knowledge and skills need to be taught in the correct order so that children begin to make sense of the subject and progress within it.

Separate subject teaching has been marginalised in primary schools for many years. Subjects have been integrated under topics or themes and there has been an insufficient focus in curriculum planning on the importance of sequencing knowledge and skills within subjects. In many instances, the primary foundation subjects have been diluted in that they have become vehicles for teaching English and mathematics.

Preserving the uniqueness of each subject is essential so that children start to understand what constitutes a subject. In some instances, children leave primary school without understanding what 'geography' is as a subject. This is because it has been integrated into a topic or theme and children have not recognised that they have been learning geography. Many children leave primary school never having heard of subjects such as chemistry, physics and biology even though they have been taught lessons which have addressed content which falls under these subject domains. Many primary school children start secondary school unable to distinguish between physical and human geography. They may not recognise design and technology as a subject because this may have been taught under the heading of 'art and craft'. The reasons for this are partly because these subjects have been given an insufficient focus in the primary curriculum, but also because there has been (and continues to be) some resistance to the teaching of separate subjects in primary schools and a resistance to the use of subject labels. The problem with these perspectives is that children are disadvantaged when they start their secondary education because they do not understand the subject labels that are used.

A curriculum for the twenty-first century should ensure that children develop secure subject knowledge and skills within different subjects. It should prioritise the teaching of subject-specific concepts, knowledge and skills so that children understand what constitutes a subject. In addition, it should ensure that sufficient emphasis is given to different subjects so that children can make progress within these subjects.

CRITICAL QUESTIONS

+ What are the arguments for and against teaching separate subjects in primary schools?

+ What are the arguments for and against thematic approaches to curriculum design in primary schools?

A CURRICULUM FOR FUTURE EMPLOYMENT

Although it is impossible to predict the employment opportunities that will be available to young people in the future, the fast pace of change and need for innovation will mean that the skills of adaptability, creativity and problem-solving will be crucial. Employees need to be able to work as part of a team. They need to be able to collaborate and communicate with others. They need to be able to regulate their social behaviour and emotions within the workplace. They need to be organised and manage their time efficiently. They need to be able to multi-task. They need to demonstrate empathy and compassion. They need to embrace and respect diversity in the workplace. In many industries, employees need to be literate and numerate and use technology proficiently. Employees need to be able to pursue, justify and defend a line of argument. They need to be resilient. This is not an exhaustive set of skills, but these are key transferable skills that employers require.

It is never too early to start developing these skills. The primary curriculum should be designed to develop these skills. It should support children to be collaborators, problem-solvers, confident communicators, inventors, investigators and it should promote curiosity. It should be designed to promote inclusive values and attitudes. It should support children to develop resilience, persevere and recover from 'failure'. These skills will support future learning and employment and they cannot all be developed through a didactic approach for teaching. Reclaiming the curriculum presents an exciting opportunity for teachers to integrate more group work and problem-based learning into the curriculum. These pedagogical approaches will support the development of critical skills.

A CURRICULUM FOR CREATIVITY

Creativity is not just about art, music, writing and drama although these are creative aspects of the curriculum. It is about finding solutions, adapting approaches and solving problems. Creativity can be embedded through all subjects in the primary curriculum. The skill of creativity is essential during the twenty-first century. Society needs creative individuals who can innovate, solve problems and develop alternative approaches. The curriculum should support children to both work and think creatively. Developing the skill of lateral thinking is one way of nurturing creativity in young children. An example of this is to ask children to identify different ways of crossing a river. There are multiple solutions to this problem, and it requires children to think laterally. Young children tend to perform extremely well on tasks of lateral thinking. However, their ability to think laterally tends to decline as they move through the education system. This is because they start to learn that there is one single approach to solving a problem or one correct answer to a question. Reclaiming the curriculum is an opportunity for teachers to design tasks which require children to think laterally and which enable them to work creatively.

A CURRICULUM FOR ENJOYMENT

Above all the primary curriculum should promote enjoyment. This is more important than preparing children for future learning and employment. Primary education is not just a preparation for the next phase in children's lives. It is a distinct and precious phase of children's education.

A well-designed primary curriculum should be exciting. It should provide frequent opportunities for children to learn through first-hand experiences. It should motivate children and get them obsessed with learning. It should be rich, broad and provide children with opportunities which exceed those that are provided by their families. It should promote curiosity and a love of learning.

CRITICAL QUESTIONS

+ Should the primary curriculum be a preparation for the next phase of education? Explain your answer.

+ Should the primary curriculum be a preparation for future employment? Explain your answer.

SUMMARY

This chapter has emphasised the role of the curriculum and has considered the implications of curriculum planning in the context of the school and its community. The key aspects of an ambitious primary curriculum have been outlined and the characteristics of a twenty-first century curriculum have been discussed. Approaches to curriculum design have been identified in relation to knowledge and skills and the role of the curriculum has been discussed in relation to children with special educational needs and those from disadvantaged backgrounds. Finally, the chapter has demonstrated how the curriculum can be used to develop employability skills as well as to promote creativity and foster children's enjoyment.

FURTHER READING

Jones, K (2019) *Retrieval Practice: Research & Resources for Every Classroom*. Suffolk: John Catt.

Lear, J (2019) *The Monkey-Proof Box: Curriculum Design for Building Knowledge, Developing Creative Thinking and Promoting Independence*. Carmarthen: Independent Thinking Press.

+ CHAPTER 2

CURRICULUM DESIGN

CHAPTER OBJECTIVES

After reading this chapter you will understand:

+ the key aspects of curriculum design;

+ the value of involving stakeholders in curriculum design;

+ the implications of the *Education Inspection Framework* (Ofsted, 2019a);

+ the importance of offering a curriculum that is broad and balanced;

+ how to approach sequencing and curriculum design;

+ how to embed language, literacy and mathematics across the curriculum;

+ the role of the curriculum in relation to social challenges, sustainability, social justice and citizenship.

INTRODUCTION

This chapter explores the concept of curriculum and, in doing so, identifies recent developments in relation to the school inspection system. It argues that these developments provide school leaders with an opportunity to reclaim the curriculum and guidance is offered to support decision-making in relation to curriculum design. It also highlights the value of seeking opportunities to involve local health, religious and voluntary organisations in this process and the importance of offering a broad and balanced curriculum is emphasised. The chapter offers guidance in relation to sequencing and the concept of the digital curriculum is also explored. Approaches to curriculum design are introduced including thematic design as well as curriculum design by subject and dualism. Finally the chapter emphasises the role of the curriculum in relation to social challenges and sustainability as well as offering practical strategies to support teachers and school leaders to develop a rights and value-led curriculum that promotes social justice and citizenship.

RECLAIMING THE CURRICULUM

School inspections have, for too long, focused on the outcomes of the curriculum rather than the curriculum itself. Inspectors have assumed that in schools where test results have been good, the quality of education is equally good. However, in some instances, schools have achieved good results in national tests, not by providing pupils with a high-quality education, but by restricting the curriculum and teaching to the test. This has been effective in producing good results but not effective in promoting deep learning. In some instances where test results have been high, the quality of pupils' learning has been superficial because pupils have been trained to answer questions on test papers rather than having been immersed in deep, rich learning. Drilling pupils to pass examinations is effective in producing short-term gains, but not effective in providing pupils with broad and powerful forms of knowledge and skills.

Reclaiming the curriculum provides schools with an opportunity for leaders to make decisions about:

+ the knowledge and skills that pupils need to learn;

+ the attitudes and values that pupils need to develop;

+ the appropriateness of different curriculum models;

+ the balance between different curriculum subjects;

+ how to sequence the curriculum within subjects;

+ how to provide coherence across the curriculum.

Schools inspections will now give greater emphasis to these aspects rather than simply focusing on pupil outcomes. The curriculum is central to pupils' education and school leaders recognise that it is a key focus of their role. No single curriculum will be perfect because one curriculum model will not necessarily meet the needs of all pupils. However, in these cases school leaders should adapt the curriculum to meet the needs of specific pupils rather than providing an alternative curriculum. In some cases, it might be necessary to provide pupils with an alternative curriculum if they have complex special educational needs or disabilities but this should only be for a very small number of pupils who require a highly personalised curriculum.

THE ROLE OF STAKEHOLDERS IN CURRICULUM DESIGN

Pupils, staff, parents and governors are among a school's key stakeholders. Often the voices of different stakeholders are excluded from the process of curriculum design. Involving various stakeholders in the process of curriculum design ensures that different individuals have ownership of the curriculum. School leaders may wish to involve local health, religious and voluntary organisations in the process of curriculum design. A curriculum working group could be established to facilitate the process of curriculum development in the school.

CRITICAL QUESTIONS

+ Which organisations could support schools in curriculum design?

+ What are the benefits of involving different stakeholders in the process of curriculum design?

+ What are the possible issues that could arise from this process of collaborative curriculum design?

+ To what extent can school leaders design a curriculum when the national curriculum already prescribes the content that needs to be taught?

CURRICULUM INTENT

Curriculum intent is part of the *Education Inspection Framework* (Ofsted, 2019a) and it is therefore an aspect which inspectors will evaluate during school inspections. Curriculum intent relates to the design, structure and sequence of the curriculum. Schools should plan a broad curriculum for all pupils which enables them to learn a wide range of subjects. The curriculum should also be balanced so that pupils can learn subjects in sufficient depth. The curriculum content should be clearly sequenced within subjects so that pupils learn knowledge and skills in the right order. A well-designed curriculum is:

+ ambitious for all pupils;

+ coherently planned and sequenced;

+ successfully adapted for pupils with special educational needs and/ or disabilities;

+ broad and balanced for all pupils.

(Ofsted, 2019a)

During the process of curriculum design, school leaders will need to decide what knowledge and skills pupils need through their primary education. Although these are outlined in the national curriculum, in subjects where pupil outcomes are less effective the curriculum may need to be modified to emphasise these aspects. If pupils are not performing well in reading, for example, school leaders may wish to give greater emphasis in curriculum design to pupils' reading development. However, this should not result in a restricted curriculum because all pupils have an entitlement to be taught the full national curriculum.

THE IMPORTANCE OF A BROAD AND RICH CURRICULUM

The use of high-stakes assessments in primary schools during the last two decades has resulted in a narrowing of the curriculum. This has limited children's enjoyment of the curriculum and has meant that many children have not had the opportunity to develop talents and strengths in subjects other than mathematics and English. Although science was designated as a core national curriculum subject, it was never given the same emphasis in schools as mathematics and English. Children have not had the opportunity to develop as scientists, historians, geographers, designers, artists, musicians, and performers, largely because inspection judgements about overall school effectiveness have been based on narrow performance indicators (ie, pupils' grades in reading, writing and mathematics). Unsurprisingly, this has, for many pupils, led to a restricted curriculum which has disadvantaged them when they have entered secondary schools. Reclaiming the curriculum provides an opportunity for schools to make these subjects central to the curriculum so that pupils can develop a broad range of interests, strengths and talents.

SEQUENCING THE CURRICULUM

Teachers ultimately need to decide how to sequence the curriculum. The national curriculum provides statements of intended outcomes which children must achieve. Ultimately schools need to decide upon the knowledge and skills that pupils need to learn to achieve these broader outcomes and how to sequence these in a logical way across a series of lessons, across units of work and across year groups.

The national curriculum statements for English and mathematics are linked to specific year groups. Schools therefore know what content needs to be taught in each of the year groups. Teachers will still need to decide how to sequence knowledge and skills within units of work and across the school year. In science, units of work are allocated to specific year groups. An example of this is 'electricity' which is taught in Year 4. Teachers will need to decide how to sequence the knowledge and skills across this unit to ensure that children achieve the national curriculum outcomes across a series of lessons. However, teaching a topic once and not revisiting it does not support its transfer into the long-term memory. There is no reason why children cannot be taught about electricity in all year groups so that there are frequent opportunities for revisiting and building on content.

The national curriculum statements for the foundation subjects are very broad and are only tied to key stages, not to year groups. Schools will need to decide what subject-specific knowledge and skills to teach in each year group to ensure that children make progress in each subject.

However well-sequenced the curriculum is, opportunities for consolidating prior learning are important. It is not enough to teach something once. Pupils need regular opportunities in all subjects to revisit and build on prior learning.

THE DIGITAL CURRICULUM

Given that we live in a digital world, a digital curriculum is essential. Technology plays an important role in our lives. We use it to study, in the workplace and to stay connected with friends, family and other members of our global online community. The introduction of Web 3.0 technologies demonstrates just how sophisticated technology is becoming. The internet is now embedded within everyday objects, a development which is commonly referred to as 'the internet of things'. This enables us to send information from one device to another, thus ensuring connectivity and communication between different devices.

To thrive within the twenty-first century, children will need to become confident users of technology. A well-designed digital curriculum should develop the skill of digital literacy. Children need to know how to use hardware and software. They need to know how to create accounts and how to keep themselves safe online. In addition, the digital curriculum should teach children the skills of digital citizenship. Children need to know how to be responsible digital citizens, how to conduct themselves online and how to treat other people online. The importance of treating people with respect both within online and offline communities should be promoted through the curriculum at the earliest opportunity. The digital curriculum should also promote the skill of digital resilience. Since teachers cannot guarantee that children will have negative experiences online, it is essential, through the curriculum, that they learn how to report inappropriate behaviour, including abuse, harassment and discrimination that they experience or witness. It is also important that children learn how to seek help when they have experienced something negative.

In addition, the digital curriculum should be designed to ensure that all children develop the knowledge, understanding and skills that are outlined in the computing strand of the national curriculum. This specifies content for Key Stage 1 and Key Stage 2 but teachers will still need to decide what content to teach in each year group. Teachers will also need to decide how to sequence knowledge and skills within units of work.

CRITICAL QUESTIONS

+ What are the responsibilities of parents in relation to keeping children safe online?

+ What are the responsibilities of social media companies in relation to keeping children safe online?

+ What are the responsibilities of the government in relation to keeping children safe online?

APPROACHES TO CURRICULUM DESIGN

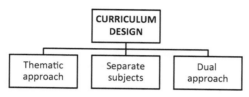

Figure 2.1 Approaches to curriculum design

Figure 2.1 presents approaches to curriculum design. Thematic approaches to curriculum design aim to bring subjects together under the umbrella of a central topic or theme. This has always been a common approach to curriculum planning in primary schools. The rationale for this approach is that it provides children with a coherent curriculum. They study a theme and curriculum subjects are then linked to the theme. If pupils are learning about the Romans, they may develop their own Roman mosaics in art and they might design and make Roman shields in design and technology. In geography they may learn about places in Britain that were claimed by the Romans. In English they might typically write a diary entry of a soldier in the Roman army. Coherence is provided because all of the learning relates to the central theme. In mathematics they might study Roman mosaics to learn about symmetry.

One of the central arguments in support of this approach is the assumption that young children do not compartmentalise the curriculum into subjects. It has been argued that dividing the curriculum into subjects is artificial because learning tasks generally do not address just one subject, they address many subjects. In an activity where pupils design and make a pizza (in keeping with the theme of the Romans), they are developing skills in a range of subjects. They might be weighing and measuring (mathematics), following a recipe (reading), communicating using spoken language, drawing a plan (design and technology), chopping and grating (design and technology) and learning about the effects of heat (science). Thus, it could be argued that young children do not compartmentalise learning in the same way that adults do. The alternative approach of teaching separate subjects can lead to a fragmented curriculum because children's learning in each of the subjects may be unconnected.

When thematic approaches to curriculum planning are done well it can be highly effective. However, this cross-curricular approach to curriculum design has been subjected to several criticisms.

+ Each subject has subject-specific knowledge, concepts and skills. Teaching through a thematic approach can result in subjects being diluted in that subject-specific knowledge, concepts and skills might be omitted from the curriculum or not taught in the correct sequence. This may result in children developing insecure subject knowledge (Boss, 2007).

+ Curriculum coverage can be patchy because themes cannot address all aspects of subject knowledge that children need to learn (Coulby, 1989).

+ Children spend a great deal of time doing activities and learning through first-hand experience but there is insufficient attention given to subject-specific knowledge and concepts. Consequently, children experience much 'doing' but may learn very little (White, 2004).

+ Subject links to a central theme can be tenuous (Boss, 2007).

+ Subject-specific knowledge and skills can be taught in the wrong order, resulting in children developing misconceptions (White, 2004).

+ Children leave primary school without a clear understanding of the disciplines within subjects such as science or geography (Coulby, 1989).

Thematic approaches need to be planned so that pupils develop key subject-specific knowledge and skills. Using the Romans as an example, children need to develop a sense of chronology. They need to know the period of history that relates to the topic and the period that came before and after it. They need to learn about the Roman army and the Celtic tribes. They need to know about the Roman invasion of Britain. They need to know about Boudicca's rebellion and the Battle of Colchester. They need to learn about forms of Roman entertainment, including gladiator fights and chariot racing. They need to know about the significance of Roman engineering, including roads, buildings and aqueducts. They need to learn about Roman architecture. They need to know about the legacies of the Roman period, including the calendar and Roman numerals. These are examples of subject-specific knowledge that children need to learn through a well-designed thematic approach to curriculum planning. If children spend all their time making Roman mosaics and shields and not developing this key knowledge, then they have learned nothing or very little. Thematic approaches to curriculum planning are useful in developing a coherent curriculum but they must not dilute subject-specific knowledge and skills.

Designing the curriculum through separate subjects can be useful in that this approach enables pupils to develop a coherent body of knowledge and skills within a subject. Careful attention can be given to the sequencing of knowledge and skills so that subsequent learning builds on prior learning. This enables children to make sense of a subject because aspects of the subject are taught in the right order and at the right time. Subject-specific curriculum design can help children to understand the disciples within a subject (eg chemistry, physics and biology in science) and the distinct body of knowledge and skills that constitute each discipline. However, this approach can lead to a fragmented curriculum, particularly if pupils are learning unconnected things in different subjects.

In practice many primary schools have adopted a dual approach to curriculum planning. This is where the curriculum is designed through themes but some subjects, or specific strands of subjects, are taught separately. In many schools, mathematics, physical education, science and English have been taught separately but subjects such as history, geography and art have tended to be taught through themes. Even where subjects are taught separately, links might still be made to a central theme where these are logical.

EMBEDDING LANGUAGE, LITERACY AND MATHEMATICS IN THE CURRICULUM

Spoken language is a key component of the primary English curriculum. However, it is an important tool for learning which should be integrated throughout the curriculum. It is important to build in opportunities for vocabulary development, discussion, collaboration and debate in all subjects. Integrating reading, writing and mathematics into different subjects enables children to apply the skills that have been developed in English and mathematics to other contexts. However, there is a danger that this could dilute subject-specific learning. An example of this is a science lesson where pupils are required to write up a scientific investigation. In this example, the focus of the lesson shifts to English rather than science. The focus of science lessons should be on developing children's ability to work scientifically as scientists. If the lesson is focused on writing, then children are not undertaking scientific enquiry which is central to working as a scientist.

CRITICAL QUESTIONS

+ How can spoken language be embedded across the curriculum?

+ Should the foundation subjects be vehicles for promoting literacy and mathematics? Justify your response.

ADDRESSING SOCIAL CHALLENGES THROUGH THE CURRICULUM

Figure 2.2 Social challenges

The primary curriculum should address key social challenges (see Figure 2.2). This will support the development of citizenship. Through the curriculum children should learn about their responsibilities in relation to protecting the environment. They should learn about poverty in developing and developed countries and understand that poverty is relative. Through the health education curriculum, they should learn about how to look after their own mental and physical health and how to support other people with poor mental health. They should learn about disease and ways of protecting themselves from diseases. They should learn to be moral citizens who understand what is right and wrong and what constitutes illegal behaviour. They should learn to treat others with respect, regardless of religion, belief or other forms of difference.

A CURRICULUM FOR SUSTAINABILITY

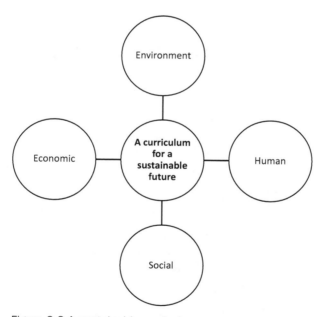

Figure 2.3 A sustainable curriculum

A curriculum for a sustainable future helps children to understand the importance of a happy, safe and secure future (see Figure 2.3). Children need to know about the importance of protecting the land, seas, rivers, lakes, the air and other natural resources. They need to know about the ways in which humans have damaged the earth and about the consequences of global warming. Children need to learn about the ways in which they can contribute to environmental sustainability and about the effects of single-use plastic on animals and the environment. Through the curriculum, children can learn about sustaining human life by taking care of their physical and mental health. Social sustainability embraces the concept of social inclusion. Children should learn about the importance of being members of a global community. They should be taught to respect people with different beliefs and about the importance of equality for all people regardless of physical or other differences. Instilling these values in children will support the sustainability of a socially inclusive society in which differences are viewed positively rather than negatively. Through economic sustainability, children can learn how to generate financial capital (eg through enterprise) as well as acquiring an understanding of budgeting, financial planning and the cost and reward of borrowing and saving. This also provides children with an opportunity to develop their understanding of credit and debit as well as borrowing and saving. These are vital skills for the future.

A CURRICULUM FOR SOCIAL JUSTICE

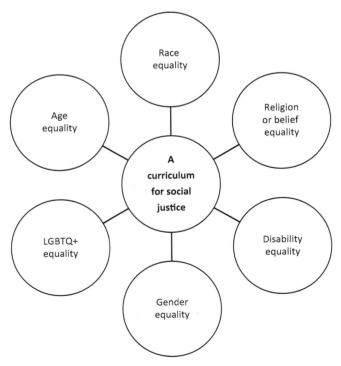

Figure 2.4 A curriculum for social justice

A curriculum for social justice (see Figure 2.4) supports children to see differences between people as a positive aspect of a healthy society. It supports children to understand (and believe) that prejudice and discrimination are morally and legally unacceptable. It should support the development of a fairer society in the future.

To support race equality, schools have a positive duty to eliminate race-based discrimination as well as promote equality of opportunity and good relations between persons of different racial groups. The curriculum plays an important role in promoting attitudes of diversity, and teaching and learning activities and resources should reflect the diversity of the school and wider community. The curriculum should also support all children to acquire an awareness of the diverse communities represented in the school population as well as through the wider community. School policies should signal this commitment to race equality and be made available in a prominent place in order to display this commitment to all visitors. When communicating with parents it is important to also take account of differing language needs. Policies should state the actions that can be taken to support this communication such as the use of verbal and/or written translations, bilingual assistants and whether another parent or community member can translate. The communication of the policy itself should also be accessible and take account of differing language needs.

The curriculum should also support children to engage in learning about and from religion. Children should learn about beliefs and practices and be given the opportunity to pose and respond to questions that concern humanity. Through this learning, children can begin to develop skills of empathy, interpretation and expression. Supporting children to acquire an understanding of religion and belief can foster and enhance self-understanding and respect for others, which promotes multicultural awareness. Aspects of equality, such as race and racism, should be embedded through the primary curriculum.

Children must understand that some disabilities are unseen and the curriculum can support children to develop this understanding. At all times staff must use the curriculum to model respectful attitudes to disability and challenge prejudice and negativity. Disability should be represented and promoted throughout the curriculum and wider school environment and key events such as the Paralympics and Deaf Awareness Week should be celebrated. External communities and organisations can also be invited to talk to children about disability, which enriches and enhances the curriculum offer.

From an early age children begin to form an understanding of gender and identity. As part of this understanding children must be supported to recognise and challenge stereotypes and gender norms and biases. If children cannot challenge these then their freedom to develop to their full potential will become limited. The curriculum must support children to recognise and challenge stereotypes and gender norms and biases and children must be made aware that these exist in the media and through advertisements as well as in branding, play and learning materials. Children should also be taught to recognise that these can also be passed on by parents and peers, as well as through communities and social norms. Throughout the curriculum, children should be provided with explicit opportunities to recognise and challenge gender stereotypes.

Through educating children about LGBTQ+ experiences and identities, children learn to respect people's differences and they begin to recognise that prejudice, bullying, harassment and other forms of discrimination are wrong. That said, we recognise that addressing LGBTQ+ inclusion is a sensitive topic in primary schools. Resistance to an LGBTQ+ curriculum often originates out of a belief that children in primary schools are too young to be exposed to this content. There is a great deal of emphasis from various groups that LGBTQ+ content must be age appropriate. However, we argue that it is never too early for children to be taught about different kinds of identities and relationships. Young children may have same-sex parents or LGBTQ+ people in their families. Some people that they know may be in same-sex marriages. They may know LGBTQ+ people in their communities. If an inclusive approach is not adopted when discussing identities, relationships and different family structures, these children can start to feel that their experiences in school do not reflect the realities of their daily lives.

Through the curriculum children should learn that people have different sexual orientations and gender identities. Children should be taught what it means for someone to be lesbian, gay, bisexual or trans. They should also learn that LGBTQ+ people exist within school and in society. The curriculum and whole-school approach should educate children to help them understand that there are different types of relationships; ie, that same-sex people can fall in love and marry in the same way that heterosexual people fall in love and marry.

When children are being taught about equality and diversity they should also understand that individuals must be treated fairly and equally regardless of age. From an early age children should be familiar with challenging negative attitudes towards age and they should be given opportunities to access resources which address ageism.

Throughout the curriculum it is essential to devise creative and respectful ways to deliver learning experiences which promote equality and diversity. This will create a whole-school and classroom environment wherein children and staff can thrive together while celebrating difference.

A CURRICULUM WHICH PROMOTES CITIZENSHIP

The citizenship programmes of study for Key Stages 1 and 2 (DfE, 2015) support schools to plan a curriculum offer that promotes citizenship. It states that during Key Stage 1, children should learn about themselves as developing individuals and as members of their communities. Children should be taught to recognise basic rules and skills for keeping themselves healthy and safe and opportunities should be offered to show children that they can take responsibility for themselves and their environment. Teaching children about their own and other people's feelings can support children to become aware of the views, needs and rights of other children and older people. During Key Stage 2, children should learn about themselves as growing and changing individuals with their own experiences and ideas and as members of their communities. Children should learn about the wider world and the interdependence of communities within it. A sense of social justice and moral responsibility should be developed so that children can recognise that their own choices and behaviour can affect local, national and global issues. Children should be supported to make more confident and informed choices about their health and environment and to take more responsibility, both individually and as a group, for their own learning and to resist bullying.

A RIGHTS- AND VALUES-LED CURRICULUM

According to Unicef (1989), the United Nations Convention on the Rights of the Child is the most complete statement of children's rights ever produced. The convention offers 54 articles which cover all aspects of a child's life and it sets out the civil, political, economic, social and

35

cultural rights that they are entitled to. It also identifies four overarching general principles which underpin these articles. These four principles are non-discrimination, the best interest of the child, the right to life survival and development and the right to be heard. Since the introduction of this convention many schools have identified as rights-respecting schools, that is, those where children's rights are learned, taught, practised, respected, protected and promoted. In these schools the community and its children learn about these rights by putting them into practice every day.

CASE STUDY

CHANGES IN BRITAIN

KEY STAGE 2

Taking a thematic approach to the teaching of the Stone Age can provide opportunities for subjects to be taught together under this central topic. For example, science can be taught through this topic with links to plants, soils, rocks, fossils, magnets, sound and light. In art children may be given opportunities to design and create artefacts including necklaces and cave art. In geography children can be asked to find out where Iron Age settlements should be located and why. To support literacy children can be tasked with writing reports about prehistoric life. Investigating prehistoric music and musical instruments can support the teaching of music and in history children can learn about changes in Britain from the Stone Age to the Iron Age. In maths there are opportunities to investigate and design prehistoric counting systems and to map prehistoric settlements using co-ordinates. This approach can help to provide children with a coherent curriculum. However, it is essential that the thematic approach does not result in the dilution of essential subject knowledge. As such, subject and topic coverage must be effectively sequenced. A strong emphasis on subject knowledge must be maintained in order to promote children's learning. The knowledge, skills and subject-specific facts that children need to learn should be identified to ensure that these are explicitly taught. For example, children should know and understand that the Stone Age is divided into three periods; the Palaeolithic (old Stone Age), Mesolithic (middle Stone Age) and Neolithic (new Stone Age). Additionally, they should understand that the Stone Age lasted from 30,000 BCE to about 3000 BCE and is named after the main technological tool developed at that time: stone. Children should also be supported to recognise that the Stone Age ended with the advent of the Bronze Age and Iron Age. Identifying explicit opportunities to teach this knowledge can support curriculum coherence and thematic approaches to curriculum design while emphasising the importance of subject-specific knowledge.

EVIDENCE-BASED PRACTICE

In 1992 the Department of Education and Science (DES) commissioned a report to make recommendations about curriculum organisation. In many ways the educational offer has changed significantly since the publication of this report. However, its underlying principles in relation to curriculum organisation remain relevant and are worth considering. According to the report's authors, Alexander, Rose and Woodhead:

If it can be shown that the topic approach allows the pupil both to make acceptable progress within the different subjects of the National curriculum and to explore the relationships between them, then the case for such an approach is strong on both pedagogic and logistical grounds. If, however, the result is that the differences between subjects are extinguished, then the strategy is indefensible.

(1992, p 22)

In the report it is made clear that it is essential that schemes of work are well documented with clear reference to subject content, knowledge and skills. Without this, subject coherence can be lost in the attempt to subsume too much into a central theme or topic. The use of topic frameworks can also be helpful to support subject coherence. These map the curriculum in relation to the subjects involved. In doing so, this approach moves away from divergent topics (which offer children considerable freedom to follow their own interests) to broad-based topics (where a generic theme such as 'Tomorrow's World' can be used to bring together content and skills from several subjects) and subject-focused topics (where children focus on one specific subject but may study relevant material from other subjects) (DES, 1992).

With this in mind it is clear that there is no one-size-fits-all approach to curriculum design. What is also clear is that regardless of approach children's learning will only be maximised when the requirements of each subject are dealt with in a way that is both clear and systematic. This means that curriculum design decisions must be made in the context of the school environment. In all cases, they should support teachers and children to maximise opportunities for learning whilst maintaining curriculum breadth, balance and consistency.

CASE STUDY

THE GREAT FIRE OF LONDON

KEY STAGE 1

Using thematic curriculum design to teach the Great Fire of London provides opportunities to teach several subjects under the umbrella of this single topic. For example, in art children can study the buildings of the period and then design and create their own. In music they can learn rhymes and songs from this period and make prints and clay sculptures of St Paul's Cathedral. In English children can write diaries from the perspectives of key people, such as Samuel Pepys, and write a non-chronological report on the Great Fire. In geography children can learn about the capital and other famous buildings in London. In history children can learn about periods of history and the period that the Great Fire of London relates to.

However, it is essential that this thematic approach does not extinguish (DES, 1992) or dilute subject-specific skills and knowledge. Identifying subject-specific skills and knowledge prior to teaching this topic thematically will support the explicit teaching of crucial subject knowledge. This includes the following.

+ When and where the fire started (2 September 1666 in Thomas Farriner's bakery on Pudding Lane).

+ Why the fire started (baking fires were not extinguished properly).

+ Why the fire spread so quickly (buildings were made of wood and straw and were close together, plus they had dried out following a hot and dry summer; strong winds also helped the fire spread).

+ How people attempted to put out the fire (using leather buckets and water squirts as well as King Charles II ordering buildings to be pulled down and destroyed to stop the fire spreading).

+ How and when the fire was finally extinguished (wind dies down by 6 September which meant that flames could be successfully extinguished.

+ Key vocabulary (including bakery, leather bucket, Tower of London, axe, water squirt, fire hook, extinguished, flammable, St Paul's Cathedral and firebreak).

+ Key people (such as Samuel Pepys, Thomas Farriner and King Charles II) and their roles.

+ Key chronology, including:
  - 2 September, when the fire started at 1am;
  - 3 September, when the fire approached the Tower of London;
  - 4 September, when St Paul's Cathedral was destroyed;
  - 5 September, when wind dies down and the fire spread started to slow;
  - 6 September, when the fire was extinguished.

+ The effects of the fire and its impact on homelessness and housing.

EVIDENCE-BASED PRACTICE

In 2008, Sir Jim Rose undertook an independent review of the primary curriculum. His recommendations were informed by information that was gathered from visits to schools, consultation conferences, evidence of international best practice and meetings with expert groups as well as a wide range of responses which were received following the publication of the interim report. The report recommends that essential knowledge, key skills and understanding of the primary curriculum should be organised into six separate areas of learning (Rose, 2008). These are:

+ understanding English, communication and languages;

+ mathematical understanding;

+ scientific and technological understanding;

+ historical, geographical and social understanding;

+ understanding physical development, health and well-being;

+ understanding the arts.

The report argues that this approach will support schools to teach a curriculum that secures essential knowledge and skills, develops understanding and builds capabilities and good attitudes to learning. Equally, it is important to recognise that the report emphasises that these proposed areas of learning are not rigid structures and that there is still scope for disciplined curriculum innovation as well as curriculum design at a local level. This means that it is still powerful for children to use and apply their knowledge and skills across subjects. As such, disciplines are clearly important in their own right but can also be used to add value to cross-curricular studies.

SUMMARY

This chapter has explored the concept of curriculum and it has outlined approaches to curriculum design including thematic design and design by subject and dualism. Recent developments in relation to the school inspection system have been identified and their implications discussed. The role of key stakeholders has been highlighted and outlined in relation to curriculum design and guidance has been provided on sequencing and the digital curriculum. The chapter has also emphasised the role of the curriculum in relation to social challenges and sustainability as well as rights and values, social justice and citizenship.

FURTHER READING

Blatchford, R (2019) *The Primary Curriculum Leader's Handbook.* Woodbridge: John Catt.

Male, B (2012) *The Primary Curriculum Design Handbook: Preparing Our Children for the Twenty-First Century.* London: Continuum International Publishing Group.

✚ CHAPTER 3
BUILDING CULTURAL CAPITAL INTO THE CURRICULUM

CHAPTER OBJECTIVES

After reading this chapter you will understand:

+ the key aspects of cultural capital;
+ the importance of embedding cultural capital into the curriculum;
+ how to develop children's linguistic capital;
+ how to build cultural capital into specific subjects;
+ the role of the co-curriculum in relation to cultural capital.

INTRODUCTION

This chapter draws on Pierre Bourdieu's (1930–2002) conceptualisation of cultural capital within the context of equality. It outlines Bourdieu's understanding of the role of the family in relation to cultural capital and it explores the association between cultural capital, social class and social mobility. The three forms of cultural capital are then outlined and examples of each are discussed. This discussion is summarised in order to provide you with a broad and holistic understanding of the concept of cultural capital. The chapter also explores how opportunities for children to participate in the arts, literature and music can differ according to socio-economic background and how this can affect educational outcomes and career progression prospects. In doing so, it emphasises the importance of embedding cultural capital into the curriculum in order to close the gap and ensure that forms of cultural capital are available to all children, regardless of their social background. Research is outlined to demonstrate the relationship between language learning and socio-economic status and practical guidance is offered to support you to embed cultural capital in a range of subject areas. Finally, we discuss the importance of extra-curricular activities within the context of the co-curriculum and we highlight how schools can compensate for disadvantage by providing these activities.

WHAT IS CULTURAL CAPITAL?

Pierre Bourdieu (1930–2002) was interested in how cultural capital is a source of inequality. Bourdieu defined cultural capital as familiarity with what might be referred to as 'high culture'. According to Bourdieu, the family plays a critical role in transmitting cultural capital through immersing children in dance and music, visiting theatres, galleries and historic sites, and by introducing them to literature and art. Cultural capital has traditionally been associated with social class. The more cultural capital a person possesses, the greater chance they have of achieving social mobility.

According to Bourdieu, cultural capital exists in three forms: embodied, objectified and institutional (see Figure 3.1). Embodied cultural capital is acquired over time through a process of socialisation. An example of embodied cultural capital is accent. A person's accent can restrict or support their chances of achieving social mobility. Another example is vocabulary. The more advanced one's vocabulary, the greater their chances of achieving social mobility. Individuals are socialised into

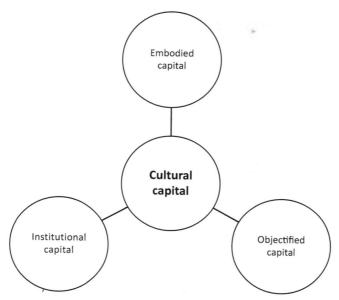

Figure 3.1 Cultural capital

specific ways of thinking or behaving to fit in with the social norms and expectations of a particular social group.

Objectified cultural capital is demonstrated through a person's possessions because cultural capital can be exchanged for economic capital. People can demonstrate their cultural capital through purchasing possessions and these can be exchanged for economic capital.

Institutional cultural capital is related to the type of school someone attends or their qualifications. Someone with a degree possesses more cultural capital than someone without a degree and someone with a postgraduate degree holds more cultural capital than someone with an undergraduate degree. Someone who attends an independent school holds more cultural capital than someone who attends a state school. They are more likely to enter Russell Group universities than students who attend state schools. These forms of cultural capital can be exchanged for economic capital after leaving education.

Broadly, cultural capital is the accumulation of knowledge, attitudes, habits, language and possessions that enables individuals to demonstrate their cultural competence and social status. Cultural capital can also be demonstrated through social interests. For example, people with greater cultural capital may develop social interests different from those with less cultural capital.

CRITICAL QUESTIONS

+ Do you agree that the emphasis on cultural capital is a rejection of working-class cultures and values? Justify your response.

+ Why do you think cultural capital plays an important role in achieving social mobility?

WHY IS CULTURAL CAPITAL IMPORTANT?

Children from higher socio-economic backgrounds benefit significantly from the cultural capital that is transmitted to them by their families. They have greater opportunities to participate in the arts, literature and music because greater economic capital enables families to purchase cultural capital. Children from more affluent backgrounds may have greater opportunities, benefit from private tuition and are more likely to attend a good school. This means that children from lower socio-economic backgrounds are less likely to experience these opportunities because families may not have the economic capital that is needed to purchase these forms of capital. This disadvantages them because they are then less likely to achieve the same educational outcomes as their more affluent peers and therefore are less likely to attend a good university and enter a high-salaried profession in the future.

Embedding cultural capital into the curriculum is a way of closing the gap by ensuring that forms of cultural capital are available to all children, irrespective of their social background. All children should have the same opportunities in society to achieve their full potential. Children's life chances should not be determined by their socio-economic background. Their futures should not be determined by the families and communities that they are born into. If cultural capital increases the likelihood of future success, then this must be made available to everyone and not just to the few.

All children should have the same opportunities to develop a rich vocabulary. All deserve to learn about the arts, history and literature. Every child should have an equal opportunity to learn to play a musical instrument. All children should have the same chance of achieving good educational outcomes. Children should not be disadvantaged because their families have not been able to purchase cultural capital. Regardless of social background, all children should have the same opportunity to attend a good university, where they can gain qualifications which enable them to access top professions including medicine, law, politics, science and teaching. Building cultural capital into the curriculum is a way of compensating for the disadvantage that may result from children being born into lower socio-economic backgrounds.

EVIDENCE-BASED PRACTICE

Research has found that social background influences levels of parental interest and participation in education. Financial capital can be exchanged for cultural capital, with parents from higher socio-economic groups being able to purchase forms of cultural capital for their children.

+ Families show significant inequalities in the power of parents to promote the educational success of their children.

+ Parents in higher socioeconomic groups were much more likely to report a variety of strategies to gain access to their preferred school.

+ Parents with higher socioeconomic backgrounds were more likely to research the school thoroughly before making a choice of school for their child.

+ Parents from higher socioeconomic backgrounds were five times more likely to report that their children had received private tuition.

+ Parents from higher socioeconomic backgrounds were more likely to become school governors or trustees of multi-academy trusts.

(Montacute and Cullinane, 2018)

CRITICAL QUESTIONS

+ How do the effects of social disadvantage affect a child's life chances?

+ How far can schools compensate for the effects of social disadvantage?

CASE STUDY

BUILDING CULTURAL CAPITAL

EARLY YEARS FOUNDATION STAGE

Schools should provide a rich and broad curriculum in order to build cultural capital. In the early years setting, children arrive with a number of experiences and ideas based on and shaped by their own personal circumstances. Using your knowledge of the children and these circumstances will allow you to plan activities and learning opportunities across the Early Years Foundation Stage (EYFS) curriculum. This should include providing plenty of opportunities for children to explore new activities through lunchtime and after-school clubs in order to facilitate questioning, curiosity and creativity. For example, offering Taekwondo training can promote discussion in relation to language and culture as well as the history of sport and exercise. Offering yoga sessions can support children to engage in discussion about physical and mental health and well-being. In some cases, sessions can be led internally and in other cases it can be helpful to secure the support of external providers. In all cases, the opportunities offered should be responsive to children's individual needs and circumstances.

LINGUISTIC CAPITAL

Research has, for a long time, demonstrated the relationship between language learning and socio-economic status. Findings indicate that:

+ children from disadvantaged families start school with lower language and cognitive skills than those from more advantaged families;

+ parents who experience stress provide less adequate social and cognitive stimulation, thus reducing the quality of parent–child interaction;

+ significant differences in both vocabulary learning and language processing efficiency were already present by 18 months;

+ there is a six month gap emerging between toddlers with higher and lower socio-economic status by 24 months;

+ deficiency in language learning can result in potentially important long-term consequences.

(Fernald et al, 2013)

Language development underpins development in reading and writing. In addition, it impacts children's cognitive development because children with impaired linguistic comprehension are disadvantaged in understanding language use across the curriculum. Children with speech and language difficulties may need a structured intervention programme to support their speech, language and communication skills. They may need a structured programme to support their vocabulary development. All children will greatly benefit from the explicit teaching of vocabulary in all subjects. Teachers should introduce children to an extensive range of sophisticated vocabulary so that they can communicate with a range of people in both formal and informal contexts.

It is sadly the case that society makes judgements on people based on their vocabulary use and skills in articulation and pronunciation. Incorrect associations are made between people's use of vocabulary and their general intelligence. This can result in people with restricted vocabularies from being disadvantaged from opportunities that people with more extensive vocabularies can benefit from. In addition, vocabulary use can also lead to social exclusion in that people with more restricted vocabularies may be excluded from social networks which can also serve to limit their opportunities. Schools can compensate for the vocabulary gap by explicitly introducing children to more complex sophisticated vocabulary so that they can fully comprehend what they hear and read and so that they can interact with people from different social backgrounds.

BUILDING CULTURAL CAPITAL INTO ENGLISH

Through English, children should be introduced to classic works of fiction and poetry and they should be introduced to significant children's authors, including contemporary authors and those who are no longer alive but have left a legacy through their works. Through reading, children can develop a rich repertoire of vocabulary which they can use in their writing and spoken language. Children should be introduced to vocabulary that is both unfamiliar to them and sophisticated. Whole-class guided reading sessions can focus on the use of specific vocabulary in texts and children in Key Stage 2 should be supported to use a thesaurus to extend their vocabulary. Children should learn about registers of speech. This will enable them to adapt their language use

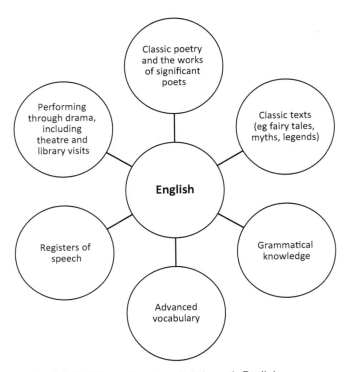

Figure 3.2 Building cultural capital through English

in different contexts. Children should learn to switch from informal to formal language according to the context. This will support them throughout their education and throughout their life.

English should promote a love of reading and writing. One approach for developing cultural capital is to introduce a reading group as part of the co-curriculum. Children could be asked to read a book prior to attending the group. The session can be designed to facilitate discussion and debate about the text. In addition, all schools should have a library which has a rich selection of fiction, non-fiction and poetry texts. Where possible schools should facilitate visits to community libraries and to the theatre. Author displays in reading areas are a useful way of developing children's knowledge about significant authors and poets. Classic poetry should be displayed in classrooms so that children can learn it by heart.

CASE STUDY

DEVELOPING CHILDREN AS POETS
YEAR 6

The children had been learning about the use of figurative language in poetry, including the use of metaphors, similes and personification. The teacher wanted the children to write some war poems, linked to a unit of study on World War II. The teacher invited a local poet into the classroom. The poet introduced the children to a wide range of poetry techniques, including different poetry structures. They created some poems together through the strategy of shared writing in which the poet verbalised his thought processes and also demonstrated the process of editing. The children then worked in groups to create a poem and after a few lessons the children composed their own poems, which were entered into a national poetry competition and published online.

BUILDING CULTURAL CAPITAL THROUGH MATHEMATICS

Mathematics education can make a significant contribution to children's understanding of financial matters (see Figure 3.3). Children can be explicitly taught about concepts such as interest, tax, deposits and mortgages. Teaching mathematical knowledge and skills provides teachers with many opportunities to facilitate discussion and curiosity in relation to these financial matters and this can support children to acquire the essential knowledge that they will need in later life. When children are learning about the representation and analysis of data they should be taught explicitly to think critically about the interpretation and presentation of data as well as whether data may be misleading. This can also be used to support children to draw conclusions about what they see and hear in the media and on key issues and debates relating to the environment, pollution and climate change. When teaching children about speed, light and distance there are opportunities to facilitate enquiry into the solar system and wider universe to support children to acquire an understanding of mathematics as a language of science. Finally, teaching mathematics provides opportunities to embed cultural capital by exploring the history of mathematics and the contributions (theories and rules) of famous mathematicians including Pythagoras and Fibonacci as well as how different cultures have contributed to developments within the subject.

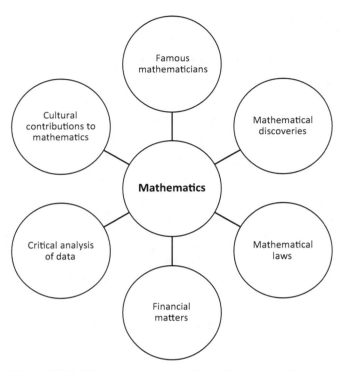

Figure 3.3 Building cultural capital through mathematics

BUILDING CULTURAL CAPITAL THROUGH SCIENCE

Through science children can learn about the work of significant scientists (see Figure 3.4), including those who are working today (eg Brian Cox). Children should develop knowledge of pivotal scientific discoveries, such as the development of penicillin and the significance of this for people's lives today. They should learn about Neil Armstrong and the work of Sir Isaac Newton, Charles Darwin and Alexander Fleming. They should be given opportunities to visit science museums. In addition, they should explore pond life and woodland and coastal habitats to support their understanding of biology. All these experiences will provide children with cultural capital. It is essential that children learn that scientists are not just old white men in white coats. They need to learn about the significant achievements of female scientists, disabled scientists and people of colour who are scientists.

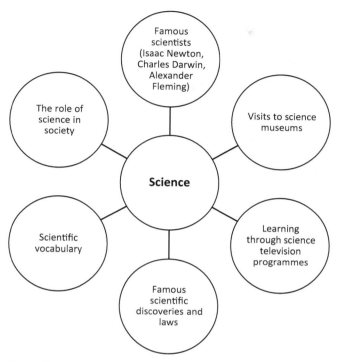

Figure 3.4 Building cultural capital through science

BUILDING CULTURAL CAPITAL THROUGH HISTORY

Through history, children can learn about the achievements of significant individuals from the past (see Figure 3.5). It is important that children understand the significant contribution that people of colour, those with disabilities and women have made to our history, for example, the work of Nelson Mandela, Florence Nightingale and Rosa Parks. Children should learn about significant events in history and the dates of these, including the Great War, World War II, the plague and the Great Fire of London. Children need to develop knowledge of chronology. They need to know the periods in history and the sequence of these periods. They should know the broad periods, such as ancient, medieval, early modern and modern, and specific periods, such as the Bronze Age and Iron Age. Children need to learn about the significance of special days including Remembrance Day and VE Day. They should have opportunities to visit historical sites and museums.

Figure 3.5 Building cultural capital through history

BUILDING CULTURAL CAPITAL THROUGH GEOGRAPHY

Geography provides children with a rich knowledge of the world (see Figure 3.6). It is important that children know that they are members of a global community and that the world is greater than their village, town or city. Children need to develop locational knowledge. They need to know where places are in the world. They need to understand how to use maps and they need to know the names of capital cities and continents. They need to understand about the equator and its relationship with climate. They need to know about the work of significant geographers and their contribution to the subject.

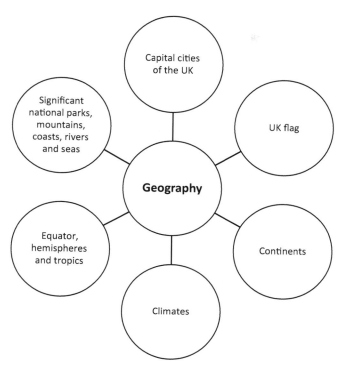

Figure 3.6 Building cultural capital through geography

BUILDING CULTURAL CAPITAL THROUGH MUSIC

It is important that children are introduced to the work of significant musicians, both current and from ages past, including those of colour and those who are or were disabled. Cultural capital in music (see Figure 3.7) includes learning about classical music and famous musicians and composers. Children also need to learn about musical genres, such as classical music, rock, pop and jazz. Cultural capital in music should develop children's knowledge of musical notation, learning to play an instrument, having access to specialist music tuition and learning songs which have stood the test of time.

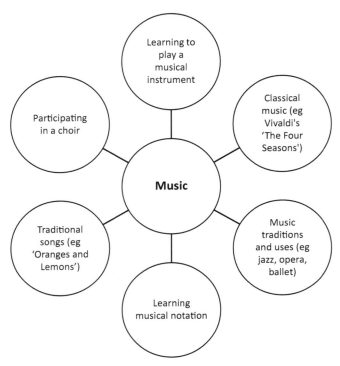

Figure 3.7 Building cultural capital through music

BUILDING CULTURAL CAPITAL THROUGH ART AND DESIGN

Cultural capital can be provided in art and design through teaching children about the lives of significant artists, designers and craftspeople (see Figure 3.8). Children should learn about significant artists of colour, those with disabilities and women artists. They should be taught about significant pieces of art so they can link this to the artist and talk with a degree of confidence about the work. Children should learn about the work of two-dimensional and three-dimensional artists. They should learn about significant sculptors, such as Barbara Hepworth and Henry Moore, in addition to the work of contemporary artists. Cultural capital in art includes visits to indoor and outdoor art galleries and opportunities to participate in art. It is not enough for children to know about art. They need to experience it first-hand by producing it. Children should learn about key genres in art and about types of architecture.

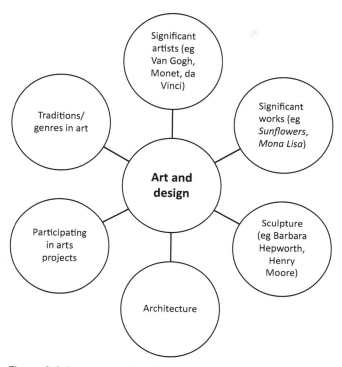

Figure 3.8 Building cultural capital through art and design

BUILDING CULTURAL CAPITAL THROUGH DESIGN AND TECHNOLOGY

There is a close connection between art and design and design and technology. Children should have opportunities to learn about the work of significant designers and craftspeople to create cultural capital (see Figure 3.9). They should learn about significant inventors (eg Alexander Graham Bell) throughout history. Children should visit museums which showcase technological innovation.

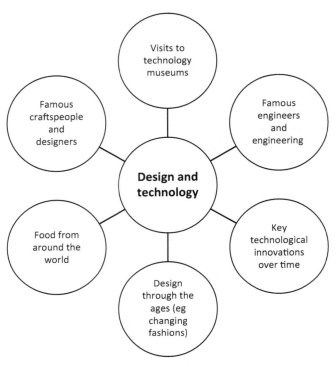

Figure 3.9 Building cultural capital through design and technology

BUILDING CULTURAL CAPITAL THROUGH PHYSICAL EDUCATION

In physical education children should be taught about famous sports people, both past and present, and the contribution that these individuals have made to our collective understanding of fitness, health and exercise. Additionally, teaching children about these individuals provides opportunities to discuss cultures and customs as well as how competitive practices may differ across and within these. Teaching children about the history and role of sporting events can also facilitate and promote enquiry and curiosity and encourage children to explore developments in the sporting world. Offering opportunities for children to visit sports stadiums can allow them to experience new things and spend time in unfamiliar settings which builds cultural capital into the physical education curriculum (see Figure 3.10).

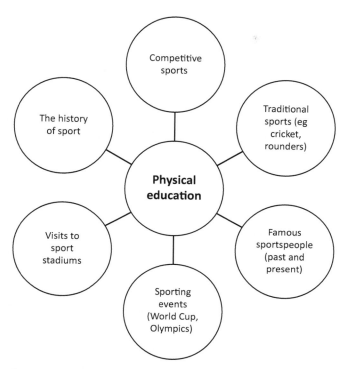

Figure 3.10 Building cultural capital through physical education

BUILDING CULTURAL CAPITAL THROUGH FOREIGN LANGUAGES

Providing children with opportunities to speak, read and write in a foreign language builds their cultural capital by supporting them to acquire an understanding of the world within which they live (see Figure 3.11). These opportunities also provide a source of cultural capital due to the economic value of language in the global market. Children should be taught about multilingualism and teaching should explicitly support children to recognise the importance and role of language in relation to culture and diversity as well as business, trade and communication. Teaching children through the use of artefacts can support them to develop an understanding of, and exposure to, different cultures. Foreign languages teaching provides many opportunities for children to question grammar conventions and this supports the acquisition and development of vocabulary and grammar in both the home language as well as an additional language.

Figure 3.11 Building cultural capital through foreign languages

BUILDING CULTURAL CAPITAL THROUGH RELIGIOUS EDUCATION

Teaching children about the association between food, clothing and religion supports them to understand how their individual customs, beliefs and values may differ from others. This prepares children for life as a global citizen with an awareness and understanding of the wider world within which they will live and operate. Explicitly teaching children about beliefs and religions, as well as beliefs within different religions, will promote children's questioning and curiosity and an appreciation of diverse views and the rule of law, liberty, respect and tolerance. Using stories to teach religious education (RE) can provide opportunities for children to engage with and understand the lives of others in a way that they can understand. Children should be taught to understand the concept of symbolism and its role within religion so that they understand the importance of pictorial representation and the origins of religious values and beliefs. Using religious texts which represent different

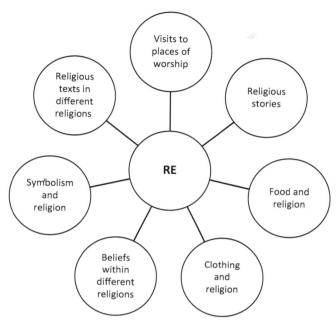

Figure 3.12 Building cultural capital through religious education

religions can support language and vocabulary acquisition while encouraging children to recognise, understand and respect difference. This gives children the skills that they will need for later life and in doing so builds cultural capital. Offering opportunities for children to visit places of worship allows them to experience new things which also builds cultural capital into the RE curriculum (see Figure 3.12).

BUILDING CULTURAL CAPITAL THROUGH THE CO-CURRICULUM

Research demonstrates that participation in extracurricular activities can increase pupils' connectedness and sense of belonging to their school (Martinez et al, 2016) (see Figure 3.13). In addition, research also demonstrates how participation in arts activities or academic clubs results in improved academic outcomes and a better sense of connection to their school (GEC, 2018).

The co-curriculum should provide children with a rich variety of activities which they normally would not have the opportunity to access.

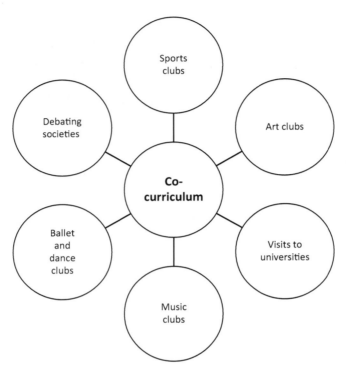

Figure 3.13 Building cultural capital through the co-curriculum

Children from higher socio-economic backgrounds are more likely to participate in a range of activities outside of school because parents can exchange economic capital for cultural capital. Children from lower socio-economic backgrounds may not benefit from the same opportunities due to lack of financial capital, which can restrict participation in after-school activities. Schools can compensate for disadvantage by providing children with activities which will boost their cultural capital.

EVIDENCE-BASED PRACTICE

Bernstein's (1971) seminal research on language use identified two types of language use: a restricted code and an elaborated code. The restricted code is less formal with shorter phrases and is used in situations where there is 'taken-for-granted' knowledge. In contrast, the elaborated code uses longer and more complex sentence structures. The restricted code does not refer to restricted vocabulary. The elaborated code does not refer to better, more sophisticated language use.

Bernstein made a correlation between social class and language codes. He reported that people from working-class backgrounds tended to use the restricted code, whereas people from middle-class backgrounds use both the restricted and elaborated codes.

CRITICAL QUESTIONS

+ What are the implications of Bernstein's research?

+ What criticisms can you make against Bernstein's research?

CASE STUDY

DEVELOPING CHILDREN AS ARTISTS

YEAR 2

The children were learning about sculpture. They had visited a local sculpture park and taken photographs of the sculptures. They had studied some of the famous sculptors, including the work of Barbara Hepworth and Henry Moore. In science they were learning about animals and in art they were learning how to use clay. To connect the different learning experiences, the teacher invited a local potter into the school. He taught the children some simple techniques, such as how to mould clay, how to join pieces of clay together and how to use clay tools to create effects. The children were then asked to create a sculpture of an animal that they had learned about in science.

CRITICAL QUESTIONS

+ Should supporting children in achieving social mobility be one of the aims of education?

+ What other aims should the primary curriculum promote?

SUMMARY

This chapter has emphasised the importance of cultural capital and within this context it has outlined the associations between equality, social class and social mobility. It has highlighted the role of the family in relation to cultural capital and it has explained the concept of cultural capital and its three separate forms. Examples of each have been offered to support your understanding of these. The chapter has outlined the importance of participation in the arts, literature and music and it has demonstrated how socio-economic background can influence educational outcomes and career progression prospects. Throughout the chapter subject-specific examples have been provided in order to support your curriculum planning and ensure that forms of cultural capital are available to all children, regardless of their social background. Research has been presented in order to demonstrate the relationship between language learning and socio-economic status and we have emphasised the importance of offering extracurricular activities within the context of the co-curriculum. In doing so, schools can close the gap and compensate for disadvantage to support the life chances of all.

FURTHER READING

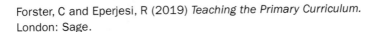

Forster, C and Eperjesi, R (2019) *Teaching the Primary Curriculum.*
London: Sage.

Yong Tang, C (2020) *Family Cultural Capital and Student
Achievement: Theoretical Insights from PISA.* New York, NY: Springer.

+ CHAPTER 4

AN ENQUIRY-BASED CURRICULUM

CHAPTER OBJECTIVES

After reading this chapter you will understand:

+ the importance of an enquiry-based curriculum;

+ the key characteristics of an enquiry-based curriculum;

+ the approaches for embedding enquiry into primary curriculum subjects;

+ the ways of supporting children to investigate a source.

INTRODUCTION

Enquiry is the way that scientists, mathematicians, authors, artists, historians, geographers and musicians work. Historians do not just learn historical facts in a passive way. They find out the facts of history by investigating a variety of source materials to develop their knowledge of what life was like. They use their historical skills to develop historical knowledge. Scientists do not repeat experiments which other people have demonstrated to them. They identify a scientific problem, they design a scientific investigation, make it as fair as possible, predict the results and record their findings. They use their scientific skills to generate new knowledge. The same approaches are used in other subjects. Geographers rely on their geographical skills and geographical sources to discover physical and human features of places.

This chapter emphasises the importance of enquiry-based learning through the curriculum. Through enquiry, children can develop knowledge through meaningful first-hand experiences. They can explore, discover and develop a sense of awe and wonder. Enquiry allows children to 'see' subjects in action. It enables them to work as an author, a scientist or a historian for example. It plays a critical role in learning, yet is often not sufficiently utilised in classrooms due to lack of time. This chapter provides practical and comprehensive suggestions on how to embed enquiry into the curriculum.

A RATIONALE FOR AN ENQUIRY-BASED CURRICULUM

Enquiry is a way of engaging children in a subject. Through immersing children in an enquiry-based curriculum they not only learn about subjects, but they also have rich and powerful opportunities to work as authors, mathematicians, historians, musicians, scientists, performers, artists, designers and geographers. Enquiry, as a pedagogical approach to curriculum delivery, enables children to develop subject-specific knowledge and skills through investigation, first-hand experiences and active learning.

Enquiry-based learning is heavily rooted in constructivist and social constructivist theories of learning. The work of Piaget emphasised the important role of exploration and manipulation of resources in supporting children to make sense of the world. The work of Vygotsky emphasised the role of language, social contexts and culture in learning. An enquiry-based approach to curriculum design enables children to learn through exploration and investigation individually and within social contexts through individual, paired and group work.

ENQUIRY IN ENGLISH

Enquiry skills can be embedded in English by asking children to critically analyse texts from the perspective of the author. Questions can be a useful way of supporting children's enquiry of a text. Examples include:

+ Why might the author have used this word?

+ Why has the author included this specific punctuation?

+ Why has the author used this specific phrase?

+ What message is the author trying to convey?

+ Why has the author used capitalisation for this word?

This process of asking children to consider the intentions of the writer when reading is a useful strategy to teach children because it supports the development of their reading comprehension skills. It helps children to consider the impact that the author intended to have on the reader. Children can reverse this process when they are composing writing in that they can be supported to employ various techniques within their writing to create a greater impact on the reader.

Children should have the opportunity to explore a range of fiction, non-fiction and poetry texts. They should be given opportunities to develop spoken language, reading and writing in a range of contexts so that these key skills can be developed. Varying this context enables children to practise the application of their skills and it promotes curiosity which empowers learning.

MATHEMATICAL ENQUIRY

Mathematical investigations provide a useful context for enquiry-based learning. This approach to learning enables children to understand that there are multiple possibilities to a problem rather than one correct answer. Examples include the following.

+ Divide 10 interlocking cubes into 2 towers to find multiple ways of making 10 (eg 6 plus 4; 8 plus 2).

+ Identify 2 numbers which have a difference of 3.

+ In how many different ways can you get an answer of 100 using addition, subtraction, multiplication and division?

+ What different coins can total £1?

+ Find different ways of folding a shape in half.

There are multiple solutions to each of these tasks. Mathematical questions are often presented to children as having correct or incorrect answers. Through mathematical investigation and enquiry children can begin to realise that there are often multiple solutions rather than one single correct answer. There is often not one single approach to solving a mathematical problem. Children should be encouraged to use a variety of strategies to solve mathematical problems so that they do not develop the view that there is a single correct approach.

SCIENTIFIC ENQUIRY

Scientific enquiry is mandatory in the national curriculum. In the current national curriculum this approach to learning is referred to as 'working scientifically' but in previous versions of the national curriculum it was simply referred to as 'scientific enquiry'.

Working scientifically enables children to work as scientists and follow the scientific process of planning investigations, designing fair tests, making predictions, carrying out observations, grouping and classifying, measuring, comparing and drawing conclusions. It is an approach which is integral to the teaching of all science topics and it should therefore be integrated into all units of work (and ideally all lessons) so that children develop an understanding of scientific knowledge and concepts through a process of scientific enquiry. It is not a discrete aspect of the science curriculum.

Through scientific enquiry children have the opportunity to literally see science happening. Many children develop scientific misconceptions from an early age. Scientific enquiry enables them to make predictions, tests things out and then reframe their initial understanding. Piaget's theory of cognitive development identified two processes which lead to cognitive growth: assimilation and accommodation. Assimilation occurs when we take in new information to fit into our existing schemas (what we already know). Accommodation is the process of adjusting our existing knowledge (or schemas) by modifying or restructuring our existing knowledge. This leads to cognitive growth because children learn that the prior knowledge no longer 'works' and the new knowledge is assimilated which results in modification of the existing schema.

This can be illustrated using a simple example. Many children assume that metals are attracted to magnets. This is reinforced through early scientific enquiry through which children explore magnetic attraction with a variety of materials (metals and non-metals). Children learn that materials such as wood, plastic, paper and fabric are not attracted to magnets but metal objects including keys, spoons and scissors are attracted to magnets. Children form a provisional schema. They understand that metals are attracted to magnets, but non-metals are not attracted. However, this is only partially correct because many metals are not attracted to magnets. Iron, cobalt and nickel or alloys, such as steel, are attracted to magnets. Metals such as brass, copper, zinc and aluminium are not attracted to magnets. Children might therefore be asked to carry out an investigation in which they are required to test a variety of metals for magnetic attraction. Due to the schema they have already formed they might predict that all of the metals will be attracted to magnets. When they investigate magnetic attraction, they will begin to realise that only a few of the metals are attracted to the magnets. They assimilate this information but it might not make sense to them because it does not fit with their existing schema. This results in cognitive dissonance or mental discomfort. The teacher can then make connections with their prior learning to help them accommodate the new information. Through effective questioning the teacher can support the children to understand that the scissors, keys and spoons were attracted to the magnet because they are constructed from metals which are attracted to magnets or are alloys of iron, cobalt or nickel. The children are then able to adjust (accommodate) the new knowledge and the schema is modified. The initial schema is likely to be established for some time before it can be modified. If it is modified too quickly, this could result in children becoming confused and information not being transferred to the long-term memory. The initial schema is only partially correct rather than being inaccurate. It supports children's early understanding of magnetic attraction and it is an important foundation for subsequent scientific understanding. As children develop, they begin to learn that they can develop a deeper understanding of a subject and that the provisional schema that they held was only a temporary schema, but suitable for understanding at the time. As children progress through education they start to learn that knowledge is temporary or partial rather than absolute.

CASE STUDY

PARACHUTES

YEAR 6

The children were learning about gravity and air resistance. They had been introduced to the concept of air resistance through a simple investigation which required them to drop various materials from a fixed height to see which landed on the ground first. They had understood that gravity and air resistance act in opposite directions and that air resistance acts against light objects to slow down the fall.

The teacher wanted the children to understand the relationship between surface area and air resistance. The children had to design an investigation to work out which size of parachute was best for a fall.

The children worked in groups to design their investigation. They spent a lot of time thinking about how to create a fair test. They understood that the different parachutes would need to be dropped from the same height, that the timer would need to be used to time the fall, and that the same object would need to act as a weight on the parachute. The children were provided with tissue paper, string, tape and modelling dough.

Each group developed a slightly different investigation, but the children understood that the parachute with the largest surface area took longer to fall because of increased air resistance. They repeated the investigation several times to ensure that they achieved consistent results. They recorded their findings in a Table and then visually presented their results using a graph.

HISTORICAL ENQUIRY

Historical enquiry enables children to work as historians. The national curriculum states:

Teaching should equip pupils to ask perceptive questions, think critically, weigh evidence, sift arguments, and develop perspective and judgement

... [pupils should] understand the methods of historical enquiry, including how evidence is used rigorously to make historical claims, and discern how and why contrasting arguments and interpretations of the past have been constructed.

(DfE, 2013, p 188)

Historical enquiry is not a discrete component of the history curriculum. It should be embedded into every unit of work, and ideally into every lesson. It enables children to develop their understanding of history through investigating a variety of primary and secondary sources. These might include historical artefacts, photographs, posters, comics, diary entries, non-fiction books, internet sources, visits to historical accounts and first-hand accounts from people who were alive at a specific time in history. Teachers can use effective questioning to support children to gain historical knowledge and understanding from a source.

CRITICAL QUESTIONS

+ What are the arguments for and against enquiry-based learning?
+ What do teachers need to consider before planning enquiry into lessons?

WAYS OF INVESTIGATING A SOURCE

Year 3 children are learning about the Victorians and are presented with a street scene from that period of history.

The children are given some time to look at the image and to discuss it in pairs. The teacher then asks the following questions to guide the children through their historical enquiry:

+ What clothes are the people wearing?
+ How are these different from the clothes that people wear now?
+ Do you think the people are rich or poor? Why do you think this?
+ What do you think people are throwing out of the windows? Why are they doing this?

+ How are the street lamps different?

+ How are people travelling around? How is this different from how people travel now? Why is it different?

The children could then be given a photograph of the same street taken in 2020. They could be asked to compare the images and to identify what is the same and what is different.

For example consider the following Figures:

Figure 4.1 Old bicycle

Figure 4.2 Chimney sweep

Figure 4.3 The impact of war

71

CRITICAL QUESTIONS

+ What historical questions could you ask the children about each source?

+ What historical knowledge would you expect the children to develop through their enquiry with these photographs?

Children often enjoy being history detectives. Providing them with a magnifying glass to examine the fine details of a source is a good way of encouraging them to look closely at an image or artefact. As children progress they can be supported to critically engage with source materials to develop their understanding of bias and propaganda. Teachers can support them to consider who produced the source and the messages that they may have been attempting to portray. Children begin to realise not to take sources at face value because they may not be an accurate representation of the past.

One of the purposes of historical enquiry is to learn historical knowledge and concepts through investigating sources. The concepts of past, present and future are critical to supporting children's understanding of time. Children need to understand chronology. In the early years children's understanding of chronology can be developed through a timeline using photographs or pictures to show the sequencing of key daily events. They can create a simple timeline of photographs which depict changes in their own lives from birth to the present time. As they progress, they can sequence key events in recent history before moving on to developing an understanding of decades, centuries and the concept of a millennium. Children can then develop a more advanced understanding of chronology once they have a basic understanding of it through being introduced to periods within history and the use of denotation such as BC (Before Christ) and AD (Anno Domini).

GEOGRAPHICAL ENQUIRY

Geographical enquiry is a key component of the national curriculum. At Key Stage 1 children should be taught to:

+ *use world maps, atlases and globes to identify the United Kingdom and its countries, as well as other countries, continents and oceans studied at this key stage;*

+ *use simple compass directions and locational and directional language;*

+ *use aerial photographs and plan perspectives to recognise landmarks and basic human and physical features; devise a simple map; and use and construct basic symbols in a key;*

+ *use simple fieldwork and observational skills to study the geography of their school and its grounds and the key human and physical features of its surrounding environment.*

(DfE, 2013, p 185)

At Key Stage 2 children should be taught to:

+ *use maps, atlases, globes and digital/computer mapping to locate countries and describe features studied;*

+ *use the eight points of a compass, four- and six-figure grid references, symbols and keys (including the use of Ordnance Survey maps) to build their knowledge of the United Kingdom and the wider world geography;*

+ *use fieldwork to observe, measure, record and present the human and physical features in the local area using a range of methods, including sketch maps, plans and graphs, and digital technologies.*

(DfE, 2013, pp 186–7)

The geography curriculum should be designed to promote the skill of geographical investigation. Children should investigate a range of maps and globes to identify geographical features. They should be taught to investigate sources such as aerial photographs to find out what places are like and to identify how places have changed. The curriculum should provide pupils with rich opportunities to investigate the geography of their local area and the features of a contrasting locality. Children should therefore have opportunities to visit places in the United Kingdom that introduce them to physical and human features that are different from the features that they see in their own locality. Children should also use a range of sources to investigate the geography of contrasting localities. These may include photographs, non-fiction books, first-hand accounts written by people who live in different places, the internet and videos. In both key stages there is a requirement to teach children about the physical and human features of a contrasting non-European country. Through the use of video conferencing software and email it is easy to develop links with schools across the world so that pupils can communicate directly with people who live overseas. One approach is to introduce a 'pen friend' system so that pupils communicate regularly with children who live overseas.

In geography children need to learn about a range of physical and human features of places. Providing children with first-hand experiences of these features by visiting places (including their own locality) provides an experiential approach to learning. In Key Stage 1 children can learn about physical features including beaches, cliffs, coasts, forests, hills, mountains, seas, oceans, rivers, valleys and vegetation. They learn about human features including cities, towns, villages, ports, harbours, farms and shops. In Key Stage 2 physical features include mountains, volcanoes and earthquakes. They also learn about economic activity and trade links. Although it will not be possible for children to experience all of these features through direct first-hand exploration, their learning will be richer and more memorable if they can actually observe some of these geographical features through first-hand experiences. Where this is not possible, teachers can use a variety of sources, such as video and immersive technology, to provide children with a near first-hand experience of these features. Children should be supported to use technology tools, for instance, Street View and Google Earth, to provide them with exciting ways of investigating the geographies of the world.

Additionally, providing children with carefully selected images can also facilitate geographical enquiry. Children should be asked to consider the picture along with its meaning and relevance and then share their findings in a pair.

For example, children could be asked to reflect on Figure 4.4.

Figure 4.4 Mode of transport

Teacher questions can then be used to guide the children through this enquiry.

+ How is this picture relevant?

+ What is the picture trying to show us?

+ How might transport have changed in recent years? What are the reasons for the change? Why is it different?

+ What might be the common problems with this method of transport?

+ Why do you think this specific method of transport was used? Was there an alternative? Why was that alternative not used?

The children could then be given a photograph of another transport method. They could be asked to draw comparisons over time or between different methods of transport. This discussion could also be used to support children's understanding of pollution and the pressures for environmental sustainability as well as advancements in technology.

CRITICAL QUESTIONS

+ What issues might need to be considered carefully before introducing a pen friend system?

+ Why do children need to learn about contrasting localities?

ENQUIRY IN RELIGIOUS EDUCATION

Enquiry-based learning plays an important role in RE. Children should have rich opportunities to learn about religions by investigating source materials. These may include photographs, drawings, religious artefacts (symbols of religions), visits to places of worship, non-fiction and fiction texts. Visits to places of worship provide first-hand experiences of religions. In addition, pupils should have opportunities to explore religious food and dress and to listen to people who can provide first-hand accounts of a faith. Children can develop an understanding of religious knowledge and concepts through the process of enquiry. Teaching should be supported by a rich repertoire of pedagogical approaches so that children engage with the subject content. Children can learn about religion through exploring art, music and drama.

Themes such as water can link to a religious story and also to geography (water shortages in developing countries), sustainability (conserving water), science (water cycle) and undertaking projects with local charities that provide clean supplies of water to developing counties (citizenship). It is not difficult to identify cross-curricular links but in doing so, the distinctive nature of each subject should not be diluted. Another challenge associated with cross-curricular work is to ensure that subject-specific knowledge, concepts and skills are taught at the correct time and in the right order. It is important that subject content is sequenced correctly and that foundational knowledge and skills are secure before new knowledge and skills are added.

CRITICAL QUESTIONS

+ What issues might need to be considered before introducing children to source material in religious education?

+ How might you teach children about the importance of respect for religion through an enquiry-based approach?

ENQUIRY IN ART, DESIGN AND TECHNOLOGY

In art and design children need to explore a variety of media, tools and processes. Early development should focus on key skills such as colour mixing, painting, drawing, printing, sculpture, collage and early photography. Children should learn about colour, pattern, texture, line, shape, form and space and the work of artists, craftspeople and designers. As children progress through the art curriculum the range of skills, tools and processes will be extended and children will learn to work with increasing accuracy and sophistication, for example, by progressing from using large paint brushes to smaller brushes which enable them to add fine details to their work. Children should have opportunities to work individually and contribute to collaborative art projects.

Some lessons should focus on skills development, for example, mixing two primary colours to get a secondary colour, learning to mix paint, joining two pieces of clay using 'slip', exploring how to blend charcoal or learning how to make a colour go lighter or darker. Some lessons should focus on the application of skills where children use the skills that they have developed to create artistic products. Children should have opportunities to visit art museums and galleries and to work alongside professional artists in the classroom. Children should also be introduced to the work of notable artists, designers and craftspeople and be able to identify significant pieces of artwork. The key point to emphasise is that art lessons should be practical. They should provide opportunities for children to work as artists.

Teachers do not need to be skilled artists to teach art well. You should be prepared to model some of the skills. However, what is critical is that you teach children about the elements of art through a combination of modelling and explanations. Children need to know how to use space on a page. They need to understand the significance of proportion. They need to understand how to use shading to create effects. They need to know how to use tools on clay to create a range of effects. Lessons should have a clear focus. Identify the skill or aspect of art knowledge that you intend the children to learn and focus on that through modelling, explanation and opportunities for children to apply what they have learned.

ENQUIRY IN MUSIC

In music children should develop their subject knowledge of pitch, duration, dynamics, tempo, timbre, texture, structure and musical notation through listening and creating music. Lessons should be practical so that children get to experience listening to, creating and evaluating music. Musical enquiry focuses on the development of children's understanding of the musical elements through music making and listening to and appraising music. Children must have first-hand experience of investigating musical instruments to develop their understanding of these elements.

DRAMATIC ENQUIRY

Drama can be used as a tool for learning across the curriculum. Drama does not have to be a polished and finished performance. It is not theatre. It is an approach which provides children with an embodied experience of subject content. It can be used within English to explore a character in more depth. It can be used in history to deepen children's understanding of historical events and it is a valuable tool in geography for exploring places or developing locational knowledge. Dramatic enquiry is an excellent approach for developing children's vocabulary and for orally rehearsing content which can later be used in a writing task. Imagine that you want the children to write a character description of an alien who visits from space. Prior to the writing lesson, the children can explore the character of the alien in a drama lesson through the use of hot seating or paired improvisation. The drama lesson will provide the children with many ideas about the alien – why did he come here? What was it like in the spaceship? Where does he live? What is it like there? What does he eat? They can develop their vocabulary through drama by learning unfamiliar words to describe the alien, for instance, hostile, undesirable, extra-terrestrial being and Martian. This vocabulary can be rehearsed in the drama lesson and children can then use it in their writing.

CRITICAL QUESTIONS

+ What other ways can you use dramatic enquiry across the curriculum?

+ How can drama help to enhance children's subject knowledge in a range of subjects?

EVIDENCE-BASED PRACTICE

Piaget (1936) was a constructivist. Cognitive constructivism assumes knowledge is actively constructed by learners based on their existing cognitive structures. Pedagogical approaches which align with this approach aim to assist children in assimilating new information to existing knowledge and enabling them to make the appropriate modifications to their existing schemas to accommodate that information.

CASE STUDY

FLOATING AND SINKING

EARLY YEARS AND YEAR 1

Many children develop the scientific misconception that heavy objects sink and light objects float. The children had been learning about materials. The teacher wanted to develop their understanding further by introducing them to the concepts of floating and sinking. The children were provided with a water tank. They were asked to predict which objects would float or sink. The children sorted the objects into two groups using sorting hoops. The teacher then asked the children what they had learned. As predicted, the children responded by saying that heavy objects sank but light objects floated.

Then the teacher showed the children a video of a large ship floating on the sea. She asked the children if the ship floated or if it had sunk. The children knew that the ship was floating but it resulted in cognitive dissonance. They could not understand why the ship was floating when it was so heavy.

The teacher then asked the children to conduct another investigation. She gave them a ball of modelling dough and asked them to predict whether it would float or sink. They then investigated their prediction. The ball sank to the bottom of the water tank. She then demonstrated how to flatten out the ball to shape it like a boat. She asked the children to predict whether it would float or sink. Despite seeing the video of the ship, the children predicted it would sink because they had just tested it in the water. She asked them to flatten out their modelling dough to create a boat-like shape. The children placed it in the water and it floated.

CRITICAL QUESTIONS

+ What did the children learn through their scientific enquiry?
+ How might their knowledge be further extended?

EVIDENCE-BASED PRACTICE

Vygotsky (1978) developed the concept of the zone of proximal development (ZPD). The ZPD highlights the difference between what children can do without assistance and what they can do with assistance. In other words, it is the gap between what children already know and what they can know when they are supported by a more able other. This support enables children to move from their current level of development to a higher level of development.

Consider the role of the teacher in the case study just discussed.

+ How did she move children through their ZPDs?

+ What strategies did she use?

+ What new knowledge did the children acquire through their scientific investigation?

The example in the case study illustrates that the teacher plays a crucial role in the process of enquiry-based learning. Through questioning, modelling and explanations the teacher can support the children to move from one level of development to the next. Without the intervention of the teacher there is no guarantee that the children would develop new knowledge and understanding.

CRITICAL QUESTIONS

+ What is the role of the teacher in enquiry-based learning?

+ What balance should be achieved between independent enquiry and teacher intervention within enquiry-based learning?

SUMMARY

This chapter has emphasised the key aspects of an enquiry-based curriculum and it has outlined the characteristics of a curriculum which supports children to acquire skills of enquiry. Subject-specific examples have been discussed throughout and we have highlighted the importance of enquiry-based learning through the curriculum. In doing so, the chapter has identified the benefits to children of engaging with an enquiry-based curriculum. These include children receiving opportunities to develop, discover and explore as well as to gain an appreciation of subjects in action.

FURTHER READING

Hill, H (2018) *A Practical Guide to Enquiry-Based Primary Teaching.* Oxon: Routledge.

Leat, D (2017) *Enquiry and Project Based Learning.* Oxon: Routledge.

✚CHAPTER 5

THE IMPORTANCE OF CONTEXT

CHAPTER OBJECTIVES

After reading this chapter you will understand:

+ the importance of school context in shaping curriculum intent;

+ the ways of addressing school context through the curriculum.

INTRODUCTION

Schools play a crucial role within the communities that they serve. Schools which develop strong links with their communities can demonstrate their commitment to inclusion and their contribution to the local context through the work that they do with families, local businesses, charities, religious and other organisations. Each school operates within communities with their own unique socio-economic contexts. The community that the school serves should be reflected in the school curriculum through its history, geography and the lives and work of significant local people. However, it is also important for children to understand that they are members of a broader global community. The school curriculum should therefore address the local context but also prepare children to take up their roles as global citizens. It is important that the curriculum is respectful of the local community, but that it also acknowledges that community attitudes and values may differ from those that are globally accepted in society. Balancing these tensions is not always straightforward and it is therefore critical that school leaders develop positive and respectful relationships with members of the community that they serve. This chapter explores the importance of shaping the curriculum to the school context and it identifies strategies for addressing this through specific subjects.

DECIDING ON CURRICULUM INTENT

The starting point for developing a curriculum is to develop a very clear statement of curriculum intent. To address this, school leaders will need to decide what knowledge, skills and attitudes pupils need to learn to prepare them for their next stage in education and to prepare them for life after leaving school.

Curriculum intent should be contextually relevant because children's needs are partly determined by their experiences of living in families and communities. The curriculum should be designed to value the local context but at the same time it should help children to recognise that they are part of a global community which extends beyond their local community. In some schools, there will be a need to design a curriculum which directly challenges prejudices which are deeply entrenched within family and community contexts, including racism, sexism and homophobia. Some children may lack the skills of independence because this skill may not have been encouraged within the family context. The curriculum can therefore be designed to promote independence. Some children lack the ability to delay gratification or to regulate their behaviour because these skills may not have been promoted within the context of the family. Others may have developed low self-esteem or low aspirations as a result of living within family or community contexts. These therefore need to be prioritised through the curriculum.

Each school is part of the community that it serves. School leaders are well-placed to identify the knowledge, skills and attitudes that need to be prioritised through the curriculum so that children are well-prepared for the next stage of their education and to take up their roles as citizens within a global society. The following might be valuable aspects to develop through the primary curriculum and might therefore be included in statements of curriculum intent.

BEING KNOWLEDGEABLE

Knowledge provides children with cultural capital. It enables them to reason and debate from an informed perspective. The national curriculum identifies the minimum level of knowledge that children need. School leaders will need to decide what additional knowledge children may need to serve them well in the future. Children should know about the history of race and racism even though it is not specified in the national curriculum. They should know about the treatment of disabled people in the past. They should know about climate change and the harm that humans have caused to the planet, including the damage of single-use plastics to the environment. They should know how to grow their own food and they should know about the importance of saving money for the future. They should know the names of the local rivers and about significant events in history which may have had an impact on their community. These are examples of aspects of knowledge that may fall outside the specified knowledge in the national curriculum but nonetheless are important.

CRITICAL QUESTIONS

+ What do children in primary schools *need* to know?

+ What *should* children in primary schools know?

LEADERSHIP

It is important to develop leadership skills from an early age. Leadership is important not just within the context of education or employment but also in the context of friendships or families. School leaders may wish to prioritise leadership skills through the curriculum.

CRITICAL QUESTIONS

+ What leadership skills should the curriculum promote?
+ How can leadership skills be developed through the curriculum?

COLLABORATION

The ability to collaborate is extremely important. As children progress through their education they will need to learn to participate in teams and group projects. Collaboration is important in work, friendships, relationships and within families.

CRITICAL QUESTIONS

+ How can collaboration skills be embedded through the curriculum?
+ What are the barriers to developing the skills of collaboration in the curriculum?

COMMUNICATION

The ability to communicate is critical because it enables individuals to socially connect with others. This is important in securing good mental health outcomes. Communication skills are critical to success in education, employment and relationships.

CRITICAL QUESTIONS

+ What communication skills should be promoted through the curriculum?

+ How can communication skills be embedded through the curriculum?

+ How can the curriculum support the development of communication skills for non-verbal children?

EMOTIONAL UNDERSTANDING AND EMPATHY

Children who have good emotional literacy are better at regulating their emotions. Emotional regulation is critical for future success in education, relationships and employment. Empathy is an important character trait which helps children to establish effective relationships with others, and in the future the capacity to demonstrate empathy will support the development of positive professional relationships in the workplace.

CRITICAL QUESTIONS

+ How can empathy be promoted through primary curriculum subjects?

+ What challenges might children with autistic spectrum conditions experience in relation to empathy?

REASONING AND PROBLEM-SOLVING

The ability to reason is an important skill in education. As children progress through education, they will be increasingly expected to justify their responses and opinions both in lessons and examinations. The ability to develop a reasoned argument is also important in relationships, friendships and the world of work. The ability to solve problems is crucial in many aspects of life and will be increasingly important in the future, given the vast number of 'big problems' that will need to be addressed in society through the twenty-first century.

CRITICAL QUESTIONS

+ What 'big problems' will future generations need to solve?
+ How can problem-solving be embedded in national curriculum subjects?

CITIZENSHIP

The curriculum should be designed to promote the citizenship skills that children need to enable them to thrive within their school and local community. Children should understand the importance of respect and equality. They should also understand their responsibilities towards their communities and other people within them. They should develop appropriate moral values which will enable them to thrive.

RESILIENCE

Resilience is critical within education and throughout life. It enables children to cope with and overcome educational challenges and other trials that they will encounter throughout their lives. Children may need to demonstrate resilience within the context of personal relationships, friendships or their family. As they move into adulthood, they will need to be resilient within the workplace. Resilience is therefore a key skill that should be promoted throughout the curriculum; the community and family context may influence the extent to which the curriculum needs to prioritise resilience. Some children develop very high self-worth as a result of feedback from significant others in their lives. They become used to being successful and they do not always respond well to challenges that they find difficult. Resilience is critical to help them face and overcome these challenges. All children need to face 'failure' and overcome it so that they can learn and develop but some children find this more difficult than others, particularly if they are used to succeeding or have been told by their parents that failure is not acceptable. Some children develop low self-worth as a result of feedback from significant others. Consequently, they may be reluctant to attempt certain tasks because they may be worried that they will fail. Developing resilience will support them to attempt challenges that they otherwise might avoid.

CRITICAL QUESTIONS

+ What factors impact children's resilience?

+ How can resilience be promoted through curriculum subjects?

SOCIAL CONTEXT AND THE CURRICULUM

The social context of the school should influence curriculum design. Some children come to school with under-developed language and communication skills, including vocabulary. They may not have been immersed in language- and communication-rich environments in the home and they may have been exposed to a more restricted or inappropriate vocabulary. These children will need a language- and communication-rich curriculum which provides them with significant opportunities to develop their spoken-language skills. Some children may need a structured intervention programme which introduces them systematically to the skills of social communication, including eye contact, turn-taking and gesture. If children have been exposed to a restricted vocabulary within the family context, the curriculum should be designed to broaden their vocabulary, thus providing them with linguistic capital.

In some schools, the curriculum will need to prioritise social regulation. Some children may struggle to adapt their behaviour to the school context because appropriate boundaries may not have been established in the home. Building social regulation skills into the curriculum is one way of addressing this. In addition, some children may not have developed the skill of emotional regulation and therefore they may require a curriculum which focuses on developing their emotional literacy and regulation skills. If the skills of emotional regulation and empathy towards others have not been encouraged in the family context, it is important for schools to prioritise these through the curriculum.

Children's self-esteem is partly informed by the views of others. Some children do not develop a positive self-image because they receive negative feedback from parents, siblings or members of their wider family or community. Developing a curriculum which enhances self-esteem is critical in all schools, but even more critical in schools where family and community contexts erode self-esteem. Providing children with a broad and balanced curriculum and tailoring the curriculum to the pupils' strengths is one way of enhancing self-esteem. Self-esteem interventions may go some way towards improving pupils' self-worth, but the best way of improving self-esteem is for children to start achieving. This will enhance their self-competence, which will increase overall self-esteem. Through designing a broad and balanced curriculum, children have greater opportunity to develop curriculum strengths.

Aspiration in some families and communities is very low. In some community contexts unemployment is high and access to higher education is too low. The reasons for this are multifaceted but low parental aspirations can have a detrimental effect on the aspirations that are transmitted to children. It is important to recognise that although parental aspirations may be related to socio-economic background, this is not always true. Some parents from lower socio-economic backgrounds have very high expectations for their children. Additionally, some parents from higher socio-economic backgrounds have unrealistic expectations for their children, which can also have a damaging effect on the child's self-esteem. In schools where children and families have low aspirations, this needs to be addressed through the curriculum. The curriculum should be designed to enhance children's aspirations so that they can set their own goals for the future. In some schools, this will need greater priority, particularly if children's aspirations are extremely low.

CASE STUDY

DEVELOPING SOCIAL COMMUNICATION AND SOCIAL REGULATION

EARLY YEARS AND KEY STAGE 1

School leaders recognise that many younger children do not have social and communication skills in line with age-related expectations. Many children have under-developed vocabulary. Communication and language skills are therefore a priority for the curriculum.

In the early years and Year 1 there is a significant emphasis on play-based learning. School leaders decide that it is appropriate to extend the principles and practices of the Early Years Foundation Stage (EYFS) into Year 1 because many of the children leave EYFS below age-related expectations in the prime areas of learning. There is an emphasis on teaching children about the rules of social communication (eye contact, turn-taking, building upon conversation) through their play and through effective adult-intervention in play. There is also an emphasis on developing children's vocabulary, both through play and through explicit teaching of vocabulary in lessons.

Some of the children struggle to regulate their social behaviour, have very poor language and communication skills and also struggle with emotional regulation. These children are provided with a tailored language and communication curriculum which explicitly focuses on these skills.

EVIDENCE-BASED PRACTICE

The 'Funds of Knowledge' approach (Gonzales et al, 2005) positions educators as ethnographic researchers. Educators research the community context by talking to community members and observing life in the community. They use the knowledge from this research to develop a curriculum which reflects children's homes and communities.

CULTURAL CONTEXT

The school curriculum should be sensitive to the cultural context of the community which it serves. The curriculum should therefore be designed to take full account of the cultural context. Some communities have strong religious affiliations. It is important that these religions are embedded in the curriculum so that the community religions are represented in school. However, it is also important that children are taught about all religions.

Cultural sensitivity is particularly important when addressing the current statutory guidance for Relationships and Sex Education (DfE, 2019a). The statutory requirement is that all children should learn about the validity of lesbian, gay, bisexual, trans and queer identities. In addition, all children need to learn that in the United Kingdom it is lawful for people to enter into same-sex relationships. This is particularly challenging for schools which are situated in strong faith communities. Parents might object to their child learning about the validity of LGBTQ+ identities and same-sex relationships on religious grounds, particularly if religious beliefs do not permit these identities and relationships.

Schools must teach this content because it is statutory. However, school leaders will need to address this in a culturally sensitive way through a process of consultation with parents. This might involve the following.

+ Inviting parents in for an initial meeting to discuss the statutory curriculum requirements.

+ Explaining how this curriculum will address the school's legal duties in relation to the Equality Act 2010, that is, the protected characteristics of sexual orientation and gender reassignment, the legal duty of schools to protect these groups from all forms of discrimination and the legal duty of schools to foster good relations between different groups (Public Sector Equality Duty).

+ The school's legal responsibility to teach Fundamental British Values, one of which is the rule of law: in the United Kingdom it is lawful for same-sex people to marry.

+ The need to respect others, regardless of differences, and the need for schools to educate children about the importance of respect.

+ The curriculum will educate children that LGBTQ+ people exist and that same-sex people can enter into a relationship and marry. It will not promote a particular lifestyle.

+ The responsibility of schools to prepare children for their futures where they will meet, live, study and work alongside LGBTQ+ people.

+ Sharing curriculum plans and resources so that parents understand exactly what their children will be taught.

+ School leaders acknowledging that they respect the religious beliefs of the parents while also emphasising that they have a wider responsibility to prepare children for life in modern Britain where LGBTQ+ identities are lawful.

GEOGRAPHICAL CONTEXT

The geography curriculum should be designed to provide children with a deep understanding of local geography. Children need to know about the physical and human features of their immediate locality. Although children are expected to learn about significant features in the United Kingdom, they also need to know the name of the river that runs through their town, village or city. They need to know how the river connects their local community to other places in the United Kingdom and the reason for the development of the river. This is one example to illustrate the significance of addressing local geography through the curriculum. They need to know the name of the nearest motorway and the name of other local features including hills, lakes and railway lines. In Key Stage 1, children are expected to name the world's seven continents and five oceans. Although this is important knowledge, they also need to know the name of their region, village, town or city and the key physical and human features of their local area. They also need to know how to use maps and aerial photographs of their local area.

HISTORICAL CONTEXT

The history of the local community is important so children can understand how their town, village or city has developed through the ages. Children need to know about significant historical events which influenced the place in which they live. They need to know about the lives of noteworthy people who were once alive and either lived in or were born in the place they live. Children need to explore the history of their local community through conducting historical enquiry. Through their enquiry they should identify the signs of the past and how these inform them today about what life was like in the past. Buildings, street signs, talking to people who are still alive about what life was like in the past, examining old photographs or diaries of local people who once lived are all important ways of learning about life in the past.

Children need to know about the contribution that the local area has made to economic development. The economic prosperity of a place may have been connected to the production of specific materials, including cotton, wool, coal, steel or shipping. Children should know about the important role of these materials in the economy of the local area and also about the contribution of farming or other industries to the local economy.

Children should learn about how their town, village or city has changed over time through exploring maps, photographs and other forms of documentary evidence.

ENVIRONMENTAL CONTEXT

The importance of protecting the local environment from pollution or other forms of damage should be emphasised through the curriculum.

This can be addressed through geography or the co-curriculum which can provide opportunities for volunteering projects. Children need to understand the impact of humans on the local environment. They also need to know about the effects of weathering on the local environment and its economy. Local geography studies can support children to understand the environmental context and the impact of environmental damage on humans and animals.

CASE STUDY

PROTECTING THE LOCAL ENVIRONMENT

YEAR 5

The children are undertaking a local study in geography. The teacher informs them that the local council has proposed the building of a new housing estate on the edge of the village. This will provide homes for 2000 families. The teacher asks the class to consider the arguments for and against this new development. The children work in groups and formulate a list of arguments for and against the new housing development.

In the next lesson, the teacher then asks the class to have a debate about the issue. The class is split into two and each group addresses one side of the debate. The children are given time to orally rehearse their arguments. The teacher reminds the children about the rules of debating before the children start.

In the next lesson, the teacher informs the children that they are going to write a letter to the local council to express their concerns about the new development. The purpose of the letter is for the children to express their concerns about the development to the council but also to acknowledge the benefits of the development. However, in the letter they will ask several questions which they want the leaders of the council to address. These include:

+ What will the impact be on the local environment, including habitats?

+ What will be the impact on traffic flow on the roads?

+ What will the impact be on local schools?

+ What will the impact be on local businesses?

To strengthen their letter, the teacher informs the children that they will interview local people to gauge their perspectives on the proposed development. The children plan the questions that they will ask and in a subsequent lesson they go out into the community to carry out the interviews. The interviews are recorded, and the children later analyse the data.

In another lesson the children write their letters to the local council, incorporating their views and the data from the interviews.

THE CONTEXT-RICH CURRICULUM

Several aspects of the science curriculum can be taught through the local environment, including developing children's knowledge of plants, animals and materials. Linking the local community to history and geography is straightforward through developing a unit of work which is framed as a 'local study'. Children can learn mathematics through the local environment by exploring shapes and symmetry in the local community. In English, children can write reports and persuasive letters about the local community. They can develop their spoken language skills through interviewing people in the community, or through leading presentations and debates about the local context.

CASE STUDY

FOOD BANKS

KEY STAGE 2

The local community has recently been affected by serious unemployment as a result of the closure of a major business. The school recognises that many of the families have been affected and that parents are struggling to provide adequate food for their children. The school leaders decide to operate a food bank scheme which runs after school. Parents and staff volunteer to provide food for the food bank which is staffed by teaching assistants and some of the children in Key Stage 2. The food bank is open before and after school. The children undertake simple stock-taking tasks and also develop materials to support the marketing of the food bank through producing leaflets and newsletters.

HARNESSING LOCAL RESOURCES

The school curriculum should be designed to capitalise on local resources. Children should learn about local artists, designers, engineers, craftspeople, authors, poets and noteworthy sportspeople from the local area. They should learn about their work and its significance. Some of these individuals may no longer be alive. However, children should also learn about reputed local individuals who are still alive and, where possible, these people should be invited into schools to work alongside children. Opportunities for children to work with local poets, authors, artists and performers is a powerful way of raising aspirations. Children begin to understand that these people may live or have lived in the same street that they now live in or even may have attended the same school, yet they have progressed to achieve great things.

The curriculum should be designed to provide children with opportunities to visit local galleries, museums, archives, places of worship, theatres and libraries. The curriculum should promote an awareness of the resources that are locally available, including the physical and human features of the locality. Children may be given opportunities to contribute to local community projects which address environmental sustainability or community cohesion (eg undertaking projects with elderly people in local care homes). Opportunities to visit local universities for aspiration days or to participate in a curriculum workshop in the local university are invaluable for enrichment, knowledge development and for raising aspirations. Opportunities to contribute to community events should be embedded into the curriculum, for example, producing food for a local event as part of a design and technology project.

EVIDENCE-BASED PRACTICE

Thomson (2002) argues that all children come to school with 'virtual school bags' of experiences, knowledge and resources developed in their lives outside school. However, only some school bags are drawn upon in the curriculum. The process of engaging with communities and experiences outside the school does not just happen, and nor is it easy. It requires a proactive approach (Gonzales et al, 2005) which positions members of the community as co-constructors of the curriculum.

SUMMARY

This chapter has emphasised the importance of a contextualised approach to curriculum design. It has identified the starting point for curriculum development and the implications for senior leaders. Additionally, it has outlined the role of the curriculum in relation to knowledge acquisition. In doing so, we state that the national curriculum serves an important role in identifying the minimum level of knowledge that children need. However, we also argue that it is the responsibility of school leaders to systematically consider and determine the additional knowledge that children will need both now and in the future. This approach to curriculum design ensures that children are given the opportunities that they need to develop leadership skills and the ability to collaborate and communicate effectively. The chapter has also outlined the importance of curriculum design in relation to emotional literacy and the need to support children to acquire an understanding of how to regulate emotion. We have emphasised the importance of children being taught to reason and problem-solve with resilience so that they can address the problems and issues that they encounter in later life. The curriculum plays an essential role in preparing children for life as global citizens and as such they must understand the importance of respect and equality. The chapter has indicated that a school's social context is likely to influence its curriculum design and we have emphasised the need to be sensitive to the cultural context of the community. Finally, practical guidance has been offered on the need to consider the geographical and historical context and how to harness local resources to support teaching and learning.

FURTHER READING

Chiarelott, L (2005) *Curriculum in Context*. Belmont, CA: Wadsworth.

Wyse, D (2012) *Creating the Curriculum*. Oxon: Routledge.

✚ CHAPTER 6
A CREATIVE AND CHILD-CENTRED CURRICULUM

CHAPTER OBJECTIVES

After reading this chapter you will understand:

+ the importance of creativity in the curriculum;

+ the role of play in creativity;

+ how to use children's ideas in the curriculum;

+ how to develop a sensory curriculum.

INTRODUCTION

This chapter focuses on the creative and child-centred curriculum. Creativity is not just about the creative subjects, although these play a critical role in fostering creativity. Creativity in the curriculum is essentially about solving problems by thinking creatively, that is, lateral or divergent thinking. Creative problem-solving can therefore be embedded as an essential component in all subjects. Society is rapidly changing. Creative people can think outside the box. They can visualise solutions to problems and develop innovations to solve them. The ability to think in divergent ways will be critical in the future for solving some of the world's 'big problems', including climate change, mental ill health and inequalities. Many of these global challenges cannot be solved by a single 'magic bullet'. A variety of solutions are required to solve challenging problems which have multifaceted causes, and interdisciplinary perspectives will also be required to solve some of the world's greatest challenges.

The ability to think creatively and be creative is also important because of the rapid pace of technological development that has already occurred and will continue to develop through the twenty-first century. Children in primary schools need to learn to be adaptable, to cope with change and to embrace multiple perspectives and solutions. These skills can be developed through a creative primary curriculum which provides children with a broad and balanced education. Creativity is also the essential lifeblood of a thriving cultural community. The arts make a significant contribution to society and the primary curriculum should seek to get children invested in the arts. It should draw them into poetry, writing, drama and dance. It should seek to create passionate artists, designers and engineers. It should develop creative scientists who can plan and design their own investigations to solve problems. It should help children to develop a passion and talent for music.

This chapter will specifically address creative approaches to curriculum planning, including the role of learning and the contribution that sensory planning can make to children's learning.

WHY IS A CREATIVE CURRICULUM IMPORTANT?

The creative curriculum creates uncertainty for teachers and children. This is because the outcomes of creative processes cannot always be defined precisely. When teachers set children a creative task, it is not always possible to predict how children will respond to the task and what direction they will take it in. This creates pedagogical risks for teachers, particularly when learning outcomes in the curriculum are set in stone.

Despite the pedagogical risks, uncertainty is important. This is because we live in a world which is full of uncertainty. The rapid development of technology in the last three decades has resulted in ways of living and working which we would not have been able to imagine 40 years ago. The economy has largely been shaped by the technological revolution of the twentieth and twenty-first centuries. We cannot predict the jobs that children will be doing in 20 or 30 years from now. However, we can predict that society will be constantly changing and that people will need to be adaptable to the pace of change. We can predict that creative solutions will be needed to solve some of the world's greatest challenges and we can predict with some certainty that multiple solutions will be needed to address the challenges of the twenty-first century. The world is constantly changing and the ability to adapt to change, identify multiple possibilities and solve problems is critical. It has never been more important than now to develop children's creativity.

It has been argued that:

today's world is uncertain and constantly changing – from shifting career and political landscapes to increasingly digital economies and social life. New technologies mean we live and work in ways that did not exist twenty years earlier. Children need skills and mindsets allowing them to step into this uncertainty, create opportunities for themselves and their communities, and learn throughout life.

(Zosh et al, 2017, p 5)

We do not tend to teach uncertainty in schools. We tend to teach children a body of knowledge as though it is fixed when, in fact, knowledge is often temporary and subject to change. We tend to focus on teaching children a single strategy for solving problems, when often there are multiple ways of solving them. We tend to teach children that there is a correct response to a question, when often there are multiple ways of addressing the question. Embedding creativity into curriculum means embracing uncertainty and accepting that there are multiple strategies and solutions.

We often think of creativity in relation to subjects such as art, music and performance. Although these aspects of the curriculum can be creative, it is important to acknowledge that creativity can be embedded into all subjects. Art is not creative if a task is too tightly defined. When thinking about the role of creativity in the curriculum it can be helpful to consider a poem by Helen Buckley. Her poem, 'The Little Boy', illustrates the argument we have outlined in relation to curriculum creativity.

The poem describes a boy who went to school. His teacher told him that he was going to create a picture. The boy was excited. He knew how to draw lions, tigers, chickens, cows, trains and boats. He was eager to get started and opened his box of crayons. However, before he could start, the teacher told him to wait. She told the children that they were going to create a picture of a flower. Again, the boy was excited. He liked to draw flowers and he started to pick out pink, orange and blue crayons to create a flower. However, the teacher stopped him and demonstrated how to draw a red flower with a green stem. The boy preferred his flower, but he dutifully did what the teacher asked him to do. He drew a red flower with a green stem.

On another day, the teacher informed him that he was going to make something out of clay. The boy was excited. He had brilliant ideas. He wanted to make snakes, elephants, mice, cars, trucks and snowmen. However, as soon as he started to be creative the teacher stopped him and informed him that everyone must make a dish. The teacher demonstrated the process of making the dish and the boy made a dish that was identical to his teacher's.

The boy stopped making things on his own. He went to another school and his new teacher asked him to draw a picture. He waited for the teacher to tell him what to draw. He did not know what to do. However, she told him to create his own picture using any colour. He told the teacher that he did not know how to do this. He decided to create a picture of a red flower with a green stem.

CRITICAL QUESTIONS

+ What does creativity mean to you?

+ What are the dangers of restricting children's creativity?

+ Why do you think that some teachers might restrict children's creativity?

A PLAY-BASED CURRICULUM IN THE EARLY YEARS

Play is critical to early learning and development. It supports all aspects of children's development. There are endless possibilities for children in unstructured play. They can make their own decisions about what direction to take the play because there are no prescribed outcomes. Children learn to solve problems and negotiate through play and they learn to use resources creatively.

Adults can intervene in children's play to extend their learning, but child-initiated independent play provides children with the greatest opportunities to be creative. It has been argued that '*the different domains of development are not silos as much as they are interconnected gears: development in one area can influence development in another*' (Zosh et al, 2017, p 8). Play supports children's physical, cognitive, social and emotional development, and development in one domain supports development in the other domains. Play also provides children with agency which is critical for development across their lifespan (Zosh et al, 2017).

DEVELOPING LATERAL THINKING THROUGH THE CURRICULUM

Lateral or divergent thinking is a term that is associated with Edward de Bono. It is the skills of finding creative solutions to solving a problem or the ability to generate multiple solutions and possibilities. Young children tend to be very good lateral thinkers but the skill tends to diminish as they get older. It is important to harness this skill because the ability to think laterally is an important life skill. An example of a lateral thinking task might include asking children to identify many different ways of crossing a river. Children should be encouraged to 'think outside the box' rather than just thinking of obvious solutions. Another task might be to ask children to think of ten different uses of a pencil, other than to write or draw. Photographs can be used to develop the skill of lateral thinking. An example is where children are shown a photograph of an old key and then asked to consider what the key might have been used for.

It is possible to build lateral thinking into all subjects with some careful planning. When children write stories, they can be encouraged to develop innovative ideas for solving problems that characters encounter. In science children can be supported to design their own scientific investigations in response to a question or a problem. In mathematics children can be taught to develop their own strategies for solving mathematical problems.

CRITICAL QUESTIONS

+ How can divergent thinking be promoted in different subjects?
+ Why is divergent thinking an important life skill?

A CURRICULUM FOR TEACHING OUTDOORS

Most early years practitioners understand the value of children learning outdoors, regardless of the weather. However, as children progress through their education, opportunities for outdoor learning can become restricted. Learning outdoors is important not only for children's mental health but also to foster creativity, enjoyment and expose children to risk. It is important that children are exposed to risk and that learning environments are not sanitised. If children are not exposed to risk they will not know how to address it when they encounter it.

There is nothing more stimulating than observing young children play with tyres, drainpipes, ropes and boxes. These simple resources provide endless possibilities for developing children's skills in creativity and problem-solving. Activities like this support children's physical, social and emotional development and help to develop skills in resilience and negotiation. The opportunities for learning are far greater when the outcomes of children's play are not tightly defined so that children can take the play in the direction they choose.

The outdoors presents a rich context for children to learn about science. Children can learn about light, shadows, habitats, plants and animals through the outdoors. They can also learn about materials through natural and built environments. Children can learn about geometry by arranging branches into regular and irregular shapes. A simple activity which provokes multiple responses from children is to provide them with six twigs or branches which they use to make a hexagon shape. The children can then be asked to rearrange the wood in different ways to create a variety of differently shaped hexagons. The children realise that there are many different ways of making hexagons and this develops their understanding of regular and irregular shapes.

The outdoor environment presents rich opportunities for learning geography. Children can develop an awareness of the physical and human features of the environment through investigating a place. They can learn about history through exploring buildings, street signs and artefacts from the past. Their knowledge of colour, pattern, texture, line, shape, form and space in art and design can be developed by observing and interacting with the environment. Through observing structures in the environment children can learn about design, architecture and engineering. There are endless possibilities.

CRITICAL QUESTIONS

+ How can the outdoor environment support children's learning in different subjects?

+ Why might teachers be reluctant to use the outdoor environment for curriculum delivery?

+ What are the barriers to outdoor learning and how might these be overcome?

USING CHILDREN'S IDEAS IN THE CURRICULUM

It is very easy to prescribe the outputs that children are expected to produce. Teachers model the processes involved for producing the outputs, and children then repeat what the teacher has modelled to produce the same outputs. This process is common in science. Teachers model how to conduct a specific investigation to answer a problem, children repeat this process and conduct the same investigation. There is no creative problem-solving in this strategy. An alternative, and more creative, approach is to start with a scientific question. The question might be: what material is the best for making a raincoat? The children need to essentially understand the property of waterproofing to address this question. The teacher might present the class with a limited selection of materials, including newspaper, aluminium foil, PVC plastic, cotton, paper, card and felt. The number of materials can be restricted if necessary. The children might be asked to predict which the best and worst materials are for making a raincoat. In groups the children could then be asked to design a scientific investigation to test their predictions. They will need to consider the equipment that they will need and how to make the test fair. The children work as a group discussing and planning their investigation. Each group might design a different investigation. The children then carry out their investigation and answer the initial question. They might also be asked to evaluate their investigation. This process takes time and may require several lessons. Teachers who are pressed for time might be tempted to demonstrate an investigation which all the children carry out. The problem with this approach is that the children are not following the entire scientific process because they are not planning and designing the investigation. Teachers may be concerned that a less tightly prescribed approach to science might not result in the learning they intended. The children could spend a lot of time carrying out an investigation which either does not work or is not fair. However, this is exactly how scientists work; they pursue lines of enquiry which lead to dead ends. The learning that arises from this process is far richer because children learn why their investigation did not work, which can lead to a deeper understanding of concepts such as fair testing.

Teachers like to be in control of children's learning. The approach that is being suggested here is a risk but it allows children to experience the process of being a scientist. It shifts the curriculum away from a 'Blue Peter' curriculum, where there is only one way of doing something, to a creative curriculum which allows children to generate multiple solutions to a single problem.

Teachers should not be frightened to give children ownership. In design and technology children must be allowed to design their own products using materials that they have chosen from a selection. The teacher might have modelled a specific technological skill which the children have practised. The children need to demonstrate this skill to make the final product. However, children should be given ownership of the final design so that the product that they design is different from that produced by other children. An example of this is the skill of stitching in textile technology. The children might have spent several weeks refining their skills in stitching techniques. The pupils might be asked to design and make a glove puppet for a younger child. Children should be given ownership of the choice of materials, colours and the stitching techniques they wish to use. Each child will generate a different product but they will each use the stitching techniques that they have been taught in previous lessons to join the fabric.

Incorporating opportunities for creativity into the curriculum gives children some ownership of their learning. It also develops their metacognitive skills which are essential for good long-term outcomes. These include the skills of planning, organisation, monitoring and evaluation. Developing these skills supports children to be effective learners because these skills are essential to independent learning. Children will increasingly require these skills as they progress through education and in adult life.

CRITICAL QUESTIONS

+ What are the barriers to pedagogical approaches which foster creativity?
+ How can these approaches be used in other subjects?

CREATIVE THEMES

There is nothing worse than studying a topic for many weeks or months if you are not interested in it. Imagine if someone tells you that you are going to spend the next seven weeks learning about dinosaurs but you have no interest in this topic. Then you discover that not only will you be required to learn facts about dinosaurs and to write stories about them, but that the entire curriculum will be designed around the theme of dinosaurs. You will write non-chronological reports on dinosaurs, you will learn about them in history and science and they will even feature in physical education. You will dread your lessons.

Sometimes teachers spend too much effort trying to fit things into a theme when the link is tenuous. An alternative approach is to teach specific units of work in each subject. However, children's learning can then become disconnected. Another approach is to follow a combination of the two approaches, that is, there is distinctive subject learning as well as a thematic approach wherein it is possible to connect specific subjects, but not all subjects, naturally to a theme.

Where themes are adopted as an approach to curriculum design, it is important to select themes that children are interested in. Children need to be motivated by exciting and dynamic activities in order to achieve their full potential. Curriculum design in the primary school should reflect distinct but interlocking ways in which children learn and develop. It should provide children with a vibrant curriculum that enhances independent learning, engagement and provides children with rich first-hand experiences. Themes that are selected as a basis for curriculum design should reflect children's varied interests and result in powerful learning opportunities.

CRITICAL QUESTIONS

+ What themes might engage children?
+ How might children's engagement in themes be influenced by gender or socio-economic background?

CASE STUDY

CREATIVE CONTEXTS FOR LEARNING

YEAR 4

The class teacher takes the children into the school field which is surrounded by hedgerows. They discuss the hedgerow as a habitat and identify animals that may be living in the hedgerow. The teacher then produces a letter which has arrived from the local council. The letter is addressed to the head teacher. The local council has decided that one way of bringing in revenue is to use the school field to create an outdoor stadium. There will be a huge stage and artistes will come and perform for audiences.

The children are excited. They will be able to see their favourite performers. The council has already booked some of these concerts and they are due to perform in a month's time. The only problem is that the hedgerows will have to be dug up to create space for the stage and the school field will be partly converted into a multi-storey car park.

The children are outraged. They are upset about the damage to the hedgerows and the loss of habitats for the animals. They are angry about the loss of their school field. The teacher encourages them to consider the impact that the stadium will have on their education (noise levels), the risk to their safety and the impact that it will have on the local residents.

The teacher asks them to write a letter as a response to the council. They orally rehearse the arguments for and against the proposed development. They then have a class debate which considers both sides of the argument. Finally, they write their letters.

CRITICAL QUESTIONS

+ Why is it important for children to have a purpose and an audience for their writing?

+ What subjects would this case study link to?

+ What 'hooks' might you use to engage children in science, history and geography?

TEACHING THE CURRICULUM THROUGH THE SENSES

Most teachers who work in special schools are familiar with the concept of a sensory curriculum. For children who have profound and multiple learning disabilities, sensory learning provides children with an embodied experience in which knowledge is developed through touch, taste, sight, sound and smell.

A sensory approach to curriculum design involves connecting the senses to a central theme or topic. Rather than making links to subjects, teachers consider the ways in which the theme or topic can be taught through the senses to provide children with a sensory learning experience. An example of sensory curriculum planning is shown in Figure 6.1 below.

CRITICAL QUESTIONS

+ What are the advantages and disadvantages of sensory curriculum planning?

+ What considerations would you need to make for children with sensory sensitivities?

Figure 6.1 An example of sensory curriculum planning

BUILDING THE CURRICULUM AROUND CHILDREN'S INTERESTS

Early years practitioners and teachers in special education are skilled in identifying children's interests and using these to inform curriculum planning. They recognise that this is a powerful tool to promote motivation and engagement. As children progress through education, there are generally fewer opportunities to follow children's interests because the curriculum is content-heavy, time is limited and children's interests may not relate to content in the curriculum.

Although these may be valid reasons to provide children with a prescribed curriculum, it is important to remember that the curriculum is not just about knowledge. The curriculum should provide children with powerful skills which support them to be learners. These skills include:

+ identifying a question or problem;

+ researching information;

+ sifting information to identify what is relevant;

+ recording information;

+ planning a project;

+ communicating;

+ monitoring outputs against milestones;

+ evaluating.

These are metacognitive skills which are essential to future success in education. Providing children with opportunities to research projects that they are interested in can develop all of these skills. It does not matter, within reason, what they research. It is the skills that are being developed through the project that are important. At the same time, because the project is self-chosen by the children, they are more likely to stay motivated.

At the start of a topic on the Victorians the teacher might begin by asking the children to identify what they already know about the topic. The teacher might then ask the children to identify questions that they would like to address through studying the topic. This is another way of developing the curriculum to address children's interests.

Teachers can find out about children's interests by asking them directly. They can ensure that there are a range of books in the reading area that address these interests. Non-fiction books can address the topics that children are interested in. Teachers might also ask the children to identify what type of books they like to read and who their favourite authors are. These books can then be represented in the reading area.

In early years classrooms teachers can develop areas of continuous provision that relate to children's interests. Areas of provision can be enhanced regularly to respond to children's interests. In the early years it is easier to abandon the planning and to respond to children's interests at a moment's notice. Imagine the scenario where a class of Reception children come in from playtime and they have found a hedgehog in the school field. When they come back to class they are excited and eager to tell you about the hedgehog. A skilled practitioner is able to seize the moment. They might take the whole class out to look at the hedgehog. The children might have questions that they want to ask.

+ Where do hedgehogs live (habitat)?

+ What do they eat?

+ Why have they got spikes?

+ Why do they move into a ball?

+ How long do they live for?

These questions can become a starting point for learning. The power of the internet means that teachers can quickly find the information to answer the children's questions. If they do not know the answers, that is also fine. Teachers can discuss with the class how they can find out the answers together. Back in the classroom the children could write about hedgehogs. They might draw or paint them. They might create some hedgehogs from malleable materials and the children could research hedgehogs on the internet. The children could learn about the threat of extinction and about societies which exist to protect hedgehogs.

These are all examples of ways of responding to children's interests. As a teacher it is important that you are flexible, adaptable and prepared to give children some ownership of their learning. Children will often surprise you in relation to what they produce and they will be more motivated because you have put them in charge of their learning.

CRITICAL QUESTIONS

+ How can you build the curriculum around children's interests in other subjects?

+ What are the barriers to giving children ownership of their learning and how can this be overcome?

MEETING THE NEEDS OF DIVERSE LEARNERS

Designing a curriculum which provides children with a range of exciting and motivating first-hand experiences will benefit all children. Children with special educational needs and/or disabilities or those who are learning English as an additional language will benefit from enquiry-based approaches to learning which enable children to learn through investigation, exploration and discovery. Learning through enquiry, through exploring artefacts, photographs, manipulating concrete resources and technology is a powerful pedagogical approach that will result in deep learning. Children remember the experiences that the curriculum provides them with rather than facts which are simply trans-mitted to them. It is important to be aware that not all of the approaches recommended in this chapter will be suitable for children with very spe-cific needs. Children with sensory sensitivities, such as those with autism, may not be able to learn effectively through all senses so this needs to be considered if you are planning a sensory curriculum. Children with social communication and interaction difficulties may struggle to learn through enquiry-based learning and play-based pedagogy if they are expected to interact in group contexts. However, they may be able to successfully learn through enquiry and play-based pedagogy individually so these approaches to curriculum design may still be valuable. Children are unique. You know their strengths and interests as well as the things they find difficult. Your unique knowledge of each child will enable you to design suitable learning experiences which meet their needs but you may also find that approaches that you adopt for children with specific needs are extremely beneficial for all children.

EVIDENCE-BASED PRACTICE

Evidence suggests that connecting with nature can be beneficial for children. Benefits include:

+ increasing physical activity (Ward et al, 2016);

+ increasing well-being (Li et al, 2018);

+ developing positive attitudes towards the environment (Collado et al, 2015);

+ developing an affinity or connection towards nature (Richardson et al, 2015).

CASE STUDY

MAKING DENS

YEAR 1

The children have been learning about structures in design and technology. The teacher develops this learning further by engaging the children in an outdoor den-making project which also links to a story they have been reading that has a cave as a setting. The children are provided with a variety of materials. They must work in groups to create

111

a den which represents a cave. The children have access to wooden poles, buckets with sand, black sheeting, cardboard and wooden boxes and other materials. They must work together to design their den. Once the den is made they are given some time to go inside to experience what it might be like to live in a cave. The children are supported to develop an advanced vocabulary by using words such as *terrified, nervous, frightened, anxious, petrified, agitated, alarmed.* The children are then given torches (to link with science) to explore the effect of light. They are then asked to write a description of a cave setting using their experiences from the den-building activity.

EVIDENCE-BASED PRACTICE

Anna Craft (2000) identified two types of creativity.

1. High creativity: this is publicly acclaimed creativity which changes knowledge and/or our perspective on the world.
2. Ordinary creativity: this is more relevant to education and recognises that everyone can be creative. Craft used the term '*little c creativity*' to describe forms of creativity which include the ability to solve problems, to think beyond the ordinary and the ability to sustain attention to a task. It is not necessarily linked to a product.

SUMMARY

This chapter has emphasised the importance of the creative and child-centred curriculum. It has explored the role of specific subjects in relation to creativity and in doing so has argued that creativity is much more than creative subjects. It is about the whole curriculum and teaching children to solve problems creatively regardless of the subject that they are learning at that time. This chapter has highlighted the importance of embedding creative problem-solving across the curriculum and within all subjects, and we have provided examples of creative thinking in order to support an interdisciplinary approach to planning curriculum creativity. We have also situated the importance of creativity within the changes and challenges of the twenty-first century and we have emphasised that it is essential that children are adaptable and able to cope with change and can embrace multiple perspectives and solutions. Finally, the chapter has addressed creative approaches to curriculum planning and outlined how sensory planning can contribute to children's learning.

FURTHER READING

Alcock, S and Stobbs, N (2019) *Rethinking Play as Pedagogy.* Oxon: Routledge.

Rogers, S (2010) *Rethinking Play and Pedagogy in Early Childhood Education: Concepts, Contexts and Cultures.* Oxon: Routledge.

+CHAPTER 7

A CURRICULUM FOR PERSONAL DEVELOPMENT

CHAPTER OBJECTIVES

After reading this chapter you will understand:

+ the key aspects of a curriculum for personal development;

+ the characteristics of a curriculum that promotes intellectual, moral and spiritual development;

+ how to promote social and cultural development;

+ the importance of a curriculum for physical and mental development;

+ the role of the curriculum in relation to character;

+ how to ensure that the curriculum prepares children for future success.

INTRODUCTION

This chapter outlines how a curriculum can address the needs of the whole child and in doing so offers guidance on personal development. It also argues that an effective curriculum is one that promotes intellectual development enabling children to acquire skills in higher-order thinking as well as application, analysis and synthesis. Guidance is offered on the role of the curriculum in relation to moral and spiritual development and examples of social, cultural, physical and mental development are provided. Four aspects of character education are highlighted and perspectives on resilience are discussed in order to support you to reflect on the role that the curriculum plays in developing character.

WHAT IS A CURRICULUM FOR PERSONAL DEVELOPMENT?

A curriculum for personal development is a curriculum which addresses the needs of the whole child. This includes their intellectual, moral, spiritual, cultural, physical and mental development. The *Education Inspection Framework* (Ofsted, 2019a) identifies 'personal development' as a separate strand which inspectors will evaluate. Inspectors will evaluate the extent to which:

+ *the curriculum extends beyond the academic, technical or vocational. It provides for learners' broader development, enabling them to develop and discover their interests and talents;*

+ *the curriculum and the school's wider work support learners to develop their character – including their resilience, confidence and independence – and help them know how to keep physically and mentally healthy;*

+ *at each stage of education, the school prepares learners for future success in their next steps;*

+ *the school prepares learners for life in modern Britain by: – equipping them to be responsible, respectful, active citizens who contribute positively to society – developing their understanding of fundamental British values – developing their understanding and appreciation of diversity – celebrating what we have in common and promoting respect for the different protected characteristics as defined in law.*

(Ofsted, 2019a, p 11)

A CURRICULUM WHICH PROMOTES INTELLECTUAL DEVELOPMENT

An effective curriculum promotes intellectual development. It enables children to learn the knowledge and skills that they need to be able to succeed in life. A carefully sequenced curriculum enables children to develop higher-order thinking skills, including the ability to apply, analyse and synthesise information. Although facts are important, an effective curriculum goes beyond the transmission of information. It empowers children to think, reason, debate, challenge, evaluate and question. These are fundamental aspects of intellectual development which provide children with the tools that they need to succeed in subsequent stages of their education and in life.

A CURRICULUM WHICH PROMOTES MORAL DEVELOPMENT

The curriculum should promote children's understanding of what is right and what is wrong. This includes promoting an awareness of the importance of respecting others, their values and beliefs, and their differences. In addition, moral development includes promoting an awareness of the rule of law and the ability to make judgements about what is morally acceptable and unacceptable within society.

Moral development includes:

+ the ability to recognise the difference between right and wrong and to readily apply this understanding in their own lives, recognise legal boundaries and, in so doing, respect the civil and criminal law of England;

+ understanding of the consequences of their behaviour and actions;

+ developing interest in investigating and offering reasoned views about moral and ethical issues and ability to understand and appreciate the viewpoints of others on these issues.

(Ofsted, 2019a)

It is important to recognise that some children live in families and communities that do not support them to understand what is right and what is wrong. The curriculum should provide all children with a clear message about what is socially, morally and legally acceptable regardless of the values that are being promoted within children's homes and communities. The curriculum is therefore a vehicle for breaking a negative cycle of disadvantage and demonstrates to children that there is a different path that they can take. Through relationships education children learn how to treat other people, including friends and family members. If children are exposed to unhealthy relationships in the home, it may take them longer to understand how to treat others. The curriculum should also support children to understand that although specific behaviours may be tolerated or promoted at home, these behaviours will not necessarily be tolerated within school or within society. Children need to learn how to treat people in positions of authority with respect and the curriculum should help them to recognise that bullying, prejudice and discrimination are morally unacceptable. Providing children with a curriculum that addresses race, disability, sexual orientation, age and gender equality will enable them to recognise the importance of treating people with respect, regardless of people's differences.

A CURRICULUM WHICH PROMOTES SPIRITUAL DEVELOPMENT

Spiritual development is not just about understanding religions. It goes beyond this. Spiritual development includes:

+ the ability to be reflective about their own beliefs (religious or otherwise) and perspective on life;

+ knowledge of, and respect for, different people's faiths, feelings and values;

+ sense of enjoyment and fascination in learning about themselves, others and the world around them;

+ use of imagination and creativity in their learning;

+ willingness to reflect on their experiences.

(Ofsted, 2019a)

Embedding frequent opportunities into the curriculum for promoting self-reflection is one way of nurturing spiritual development. Developing a rich curriculum which provides opportunities for children to become immersed in deep learning through problem-solving, investigation and collaborative learning helps to develop children's enjoyment in and fascination for learning. Activities which enable children to take risks or which promote engagement with the natural environment can also promote intrinsic motivation and a sense of awe and wonder. Providing children with opportunities to become immersed in one task or project for an extended length of time can also promote enjoyment and fascination.

Too often, children are expected to race through the curriculum at speed. There are limited opportunities for children to become absorbed in learning and unfortunately, in many primary schools, the structure of the school day now mirrors a secondary school timetable. This means that children move quickly from one lesson to the next, without any opportunity to engage deeply with a task. It is time for primary schools to reclaim the curriculum. Spending a whole morning or afternoon on a piece of artwork or writing allows children to become absorbed in their work. Allocating an entire day or week to science or to a design and technology project can provide rich opportunities for children to work as scientists, designers or engineers. Immersing children in history through drama or investigation of historical sources can foster interest, fascination and obsession about learning. Moving children on too quickly from one task to the next limits exposure to deep and rich learning experiences which children will remember.

CRITICAL QUESTIONS

+ How are opportunities for promoting self-reflection embedded across your curriculum?

+ What knowledge and skills do children need to be able to succeed in life?

A CURRICULUM FOR SOCIAL DEVELOPMENT

A curriculum for social development supports children to understand the importance of adjusting their behaviour in different contexts and it also supports children to regulate their behaviours in different social situations.

Social development includes:

+ using a range of social skills in different contexts, for example working and socialising with other pupils, including those from different religious, ethnic and socio-economic backgrounds

118

+ willingness to participate in a variety of communities and social settings, including by volunteering, cooperating well with others and being able to resolve conflicts effectively

+ acceptance and engagement with the fundamental British values of democracy, the rule of law, individual liberty and mutual respect and tolerance of those with different faiths and beliefs; they develop and demonstrate skills and attitudes that will allow them to participate fully in and contribute positively to life in modern Britain.

(Ofsted, 2019a)

Schools can build opportunities for collaborative learning into the curriculum to support them in developing important social skills. These include turn-taking, listening to others, showing respect towards other people and sharing. Fundamental British values should be promoted through the curriculum in addition to being taught in personal, social and health education. Subject leaders should identify links to these during curriculum planning.

A CURRICULUM FOR CULTURAL DEVELOPMENT

Cultural development is not just teaching children about different cultures, although this is a key component. It also includes developing an awareness of different socio-economic backgrounds. Cultural development includes:

+ understanding and appreciation of the wide range of cultural influences that have shaped their own heritage and that of others;

+ understanding and appreciation of the range of different cultures in the school and further afield as an essential element of their preparation for life in modern Britain;

+ the ability to recognise, and value, the things we share in common across cultural, religious, ethnic and socio-economic communities;

+ knowledge of Britain's democratic parliamentary system and its central role in shaping our history and values, and in continuing to develop Britain;

+ a willingness to participate in and respond positively to artistic, musical, sporting and cultural opportunities;

+ an interest in exploring, improving understanding of and showing respect for different faiths and cultural diversity and the extent to which they understand, accept and respect diversity. This is shown by their respect and attitudes towards different religious, ethnic and socio-economic groups in the local, national and global communities.

(Ofsted, 2019a)

A CURRICULUM WHICH PROMOTES PHYSICAL DEVELOPMENT

Physical development is an essential aspect of healthy childhood development. Children need to be physically active so that they can be healthy and strong. Physical activity also promotes good mental health. Children need frequent opportunities for movement and therefore physical education is an essential component of the early childhood curriculum.

A CURRICULUM WHICH PROMOTES GOOD MENTAL HEALTH

The curriculum should support children not only to be aware of the importance of physical health but also the importance of looking after their mental health. In the early stages of children's education, the curriculum should develop children's understanding of a range of emotions. It is important that children can name the different emotions that they experience and that they know that it is normal for everyone to experience these different emotions. The curriculum should also provide children with strategies which enable them to regulate their emotions.

The mental health curriculum needs to be age-appropriate. Schools will need to decide when to start introducing children to specific mental health conditions. The curriculum should help children to understand the importance of talking to others about their feelings and provide them with a range of strategies for managing their own mental health. It should also ensure that children know how to seek support for their mental health.

CASE STUDY

PROMOTING MENTAL DEVELOPMENT

RECEPTION TO YEAR 6

Monitoring and observing children to see where they are developmentally means that learning experiences can be meaningfully planned. One of these experiences is using a variety of developmentally appropriate and culturally diverse reading materials in order to model the values of care, respect and honesty. Providing thought-provoking materials supports children's mental development because it enables children from all backgrounds to experience a sense of belonging. It is also helpful to provide a culturally sensitive space for children to engage with these materials. Where possible, this space should reflect the needs and interests of the children that use it and there may be an opportunity for children to influence, design or personalise part of this space.

A CURRICULUM WHICH PROMOTES BROADER DEVELOPMENT

The national curriculum is a minimum entitlement for children's education. It sets out the knowledge and skills that children need to be taught. However, an effective curriculum enables children to develop a broad range of interests and skills. Schools should aim to contextualise the curriculum to make it relevant to the children and the communities which schools serve. Although this is a useful starting point, it is important not to restrict opportunities for children to develop a broader range of interests. A well-designed curriculum should provide children with the knowledge and experiences which will enable them to thrive in the future. This is known as cultural capital. Limiting children's cultural capital restricts their future opportunities and life chances and can result in children not achieving social mobility.

A well-designed curriculum can introduce children to experiences which they otherwise might not get. These include visits to museums and galleries, theatres, national parks, places of interest and other cultural experiences. Increasing the prominence of the arts and humanities in the curriculum can provide children with cultural capital but also improve their mental health. Every child should have an opportunity to learn to play a musical instrument. All children should have opportunities to visit a place of natural beauty and a historical site. Everyone should have an opportunity to watch a performance and to visit a gallery. Children also need opportunities to participate in adventurous outdoor activities and to develop a love of nature. Participating in activities such as gardening and cookery can support children's learning about environmental sustainability and nutrition. Through a rich curriculum, which goes beyond the requirements of the national curriculum, children can learn about environmental sustainability, climate change, poverty, financial and household management, and enterprise. Race, gender, sexual orientation and disability equality should be embedded throughout the curriculum so that children are aware of the histories of marginalised groups and are prepared for life in a socially inclusive society. A well-designed curriculum should promote social and cultural diversity.

The co-curriculum offer can supplement the national curriculum by providing opportunities for children to develop a broad range of interests and skills. The curriculum should ignite a passion for learning but it can only do this if it is sufficiently broad and if it provides opportunities for deep, sustained and rich learning. It should develop the skills that children will need in the future. These include teamwork, leadership and problem-solving.

For far too long, the curriculum in primary schools has been largely determined by the things that have been tested in the statutory assessment tests. The arts and humanities have been taught through topics or themes and the time allocated to them has been insufficient. The result is that children have moved onto secondary school and have been unprepared for subject learning in subjects other than English and mathematics. The things that make subjects discrete, the knowledge, subject-specific concepts and skills have been diluted as subjects have been integrated to either save time, ensure coverage or establish curriculum links. A curriculum for the twenty-first century must be broad enough to provide children with the knowledge, skills and attitudes that they will need in the future. It must also focus on what makes subjects unique so that children are fully prepared for secondary education.

A CURRICULUM WHICH PROMOTES CHARACTER

The *Character Education: Framework Guidance*, published by the Department for Education (DfE), identifies four important aspects of character education:

+ *the ability to remain motivated by long-term goals, to see a link between effort in the present and pay-off in the longer-term, overcoming and persevering through, and learning from, setbacks when encountered;*

+ *the learning and habituation of positive moral attributes, sometimes known as 'virtues', and including, for example, courage, honesty, generosity, integrity, humility and a sense of justice, alongside others;*

+ *the acquisition of social confidence and the ability to make points or arguments clearly and constructively, listen attentively to the views of others, behave with courtesy and good manners and speak persuasively to an audience;*

+ *an appreciation of the importance of long-term commitments which frame the successful and fulfilled life, for example to spouse, partner, role or vocation, the local community, to faith or world view. This helps individuals to put down deep roots and gives stability and longevity to lifetime endeavours.*

(DfE, 2019b, p 7)

One key character trait which schools focus on promoting is resilience. Earlier perspectives on resilience conceptualised it as a fixed trait within individuals (Masten and Garmezy, 1985). However, contemporary perspectives conceptualise resilience as a dynamic attribute which can be enhanced (Luthar, 2006; Roffey, 2017; Stephens, 2013). Definitions of resilience emphasise positive adaptation following adversity or trauma (Gayton and Lovell, 2012) and the capacity to grow in response to adversity (Stallman, 2011). Definitions emphasise the capacity to rebound from adversity and the ability to problem-solve and to return to the previous state (Sanderson and Brewer, 2017).

This ability to 'push through' regardless of circumstances is a dominant theme in the literature (Reyes et al, 2015) but these perspectives offer only a partial understanding of resilience. Resilience is not a straightforward concept (Roffey, 2017). It is a multidimensional construct which varies in different contexts (Roffey, 2017) and can change over time. Children can be resilient in one context but less so in another. Resilience is often understood to represent the capacity of individuals to 'bounce back' from difficult or painful circumstances. This is easier to achieve when individuals have access to positive support networks. Access to positive and nurturing relationships at home and in school can support resilience. Positive school cultures which promote a sense of belonging through valuing diversity also enhance children's resilience. However, some children live in households where they experience abuse, neglect, inconsistent or low behavioural expectations, parental conflict and separation. These children may find it more difficult to be resilient but schools can, at least partially, compensate for adverse circumstances in the home. Some children have experienced significant trauma which may mean that they cannot simply bounce back from this and return to their normal state (Roffey, 2017). In these circumstances, pastoral support and counselling may be required to help children.

CASE STUDY

PROMOTING CHARACTER

RECEPTION TO YEAR 6

Personal excellence can be promoted through teaching values such as respect, compassion and excellence and modelling these in all aspects of school life. Each of these values can be focused on half-termly or termly with regular whole-school assemblies and class-based activities to contextualise these values and bring them alive. Each of the school values should also be embedded throughout the curriculum and recognition and reward systems can be linked to the value system that is in place. This may include the use of stickers and certificates as well as appointing ambassadors linked to each value.

A CURRICULUM WHICH HELPS CHILDREN TO STAY MENTALLY HEALTHY

The mental health curriculum should promote the importance of physical activity and relaxation in supporting children's mental health. It should introduce them to a range of emotions and provide them with strategies for managing emotions. The mental health curriculum should help them to understand the importance of talking to others about how they feel, and it should enable them to understand how to seek help if they need it. As children progress into Key Stage 2 the curriculum should introduce children to common forms of mental ill health.

The curriculum in its entirety can support children to stay mentally healthy by promoting enjoyment, collaboration and physical activity. A broad, balanced and rich curriculum will also support children to stay mentally healthy. Integrating opportunities for volunteering in the community also supports mental health. Incorporating opportunities for outdoor learning in the curriculum can foster children's connection with nature, which also supports good mental health. Integrating mindfulness and other forms of relaxation into the school timetable helps children to take stock and appreciate the present rather than worrying about the past or the future.

A CURRICULUM WHICH PROMOTES PHYSICAL HEALTH

The importance of providing children with a curriculum which promotes physical activity has already been mentioned. Physical activity is not just physical education. The curriculum should provide children with opportunities to be physically active as much as possible. Children need to be taught about the importance of regular exercise and the risks associated with obesity. In addition, a well-designed health education curriculum introduces children to the importance of a healthy, nutritious diet and the dangers of substance abuse. It is important that the curriculum is age-appropriate and therefore schools will need to decide when to introduce children to the dangers of drug use, alcohol and cigarettes. It is also important that the curriculum introduces children to the dangers associated with lack of sleep and too much screen time. In addition, children need to know about the importance of good personal hygiene, including oral hygiene, dental health and overexposure to the sun.

A CURRICULUM FOR FUTURE SUCCESS

Ultimately, schools need to ensure that the school curriculum prepares children for future success. This includes:

+ prioritising early literacy development, including reading and writing;

+ ensuring that pupils are numerate;

+ ensuring that children have an extensive vocabulary;

+ ensuring that children know how to behave and can adjust their behaviour in different social contexts;

+ ensuring that children can regulate their emotions;

+ ensuring that children can treat other people with respect, regardless of differences;

+ ensuring that children can work effectively as part of a team.

This is not an exhaustive list. However, to cope with secondary school, employment and further and higher education, these are essential prerequisites. Other skills are important for future success, including the ability to be creative, adaptable and the ability to process multiple pieces of information at the same time. Some of these skills can be developed later but the primary curriculum should prioritise the skills that are listed here to ensure that children are prepared for their next phase of education. The national curriculum outlines the minimum knowledge and skills that children need for future success but schools are free to determine what additional skills and knowledge are also required.

A CURRICULUM WHICH PROMOTES RELATIONSHIPS EDUCATION

The Department for Education has issued statutory guidance which makes Relationships Education compulsory in all primary schools from September 2020. This guidance replaced previous guidance that was issued in 2000 in order to reflect contemporary families, relationships and legislation. The updated guidance expects that primary schools teach children about different types of relationships including single-parent families, same-sex parents, foster parents and adoptive parents. It also requires children to be taught about online relationships and how to stay safe online. For primary schools this guidance focuses on the characteristics of positive relationships with specific emphasis on friendships, family relationships and relationships with peers.

The curriculum plays an important role in Relationships Education as it supports children to understand how to treat others including the need for kindness, consideration, respect, honesty, truthfulness, permission-seeking and personal boundaries. It should also teach children about the features of healthy relationships, including friendships, so that they can identify unhealthy relationships when they encounter them. Furthermore, the curriculum should support children to acquire this understanding through sensitive and age-appropriate teaching. However, parents do not have a right to withdraw their child from Relationships Education.

A CURRICULUM WHICH PREPARES CHILDREN FOR LIFE IN MODERN BRITAIN

Schools are legally required to teach fundamental British values, including the law. This teaching should prepare children for life in modern Britain by demonstrating the importance of respect for other people, regardless of belief or identity. The curriculum should also support children to acquire an understanding of the need for individual liberty, mutual respect and tolerance of those with different faiths and beliefs. Children must understand that recognising people who are different is one of the fundamental British values. The curriculum plays an important role in teaching children that difference takes many forms including, but not restricted to, physical appearance, personality, social background, cultural diversity, disability, sexual orientation, sex, gender, age and religion or belief. Above all, the curriculum must support children to know and understand that they have a responsibility to respect other people irrespective of any differences. This principle helps children's development as good citizens and it also contributes to the development of an inclusive society.

EVIDENCE-BASED PRACTICE

Research has found that:

+ high self-efficacy, or self-belief, is associated with better performance, more persistence and greater interest in work;

+ highly motivated children (linked to tenacity) driven internally and not by extrinsic rewards show greater levels of persistence and achievement;

+ good self-control (or self-regulation, the ability to delay gratification) is associated with greater attainment levels;

+ having good coping skills (part of being able to bounce back) is associated with greater well-being.

(Gutman and Schoon, 2013)

CRITICAL QUESTIONS

+ How can the curriculum promote self-regulation?

+ How does your curriculum support children to be mentally healthy?

EVIDENCE-BASED PRACTICE

Self-esteem can act as a buffer which supports individuals to cope with adverse situations (Jindal-Snape and Miller, 2010). An individual's self-worth (how they see themselves) is strongly influenced by others (Cooley, 1902; Coopersmith, 1967; Rogers, 1961).

Mruk's (1999) two-dimensional model of self-esteem is supported by empirical studies (Tafarodi and Milne, 2002; Tafarodi and Swann, 1995). The model identifies two components of self-esteem; *self-worth* and *self-competence*. According to this model self-esteem is conceptualised as the integrated sum of these two components (Jindal-Snape and Miller, 2010). Self-worth is an individual's appraisal of themselves based on other people's evaluations of them and self-competence refers to an individual's sense of their ability to meet the challenges that they face in life (Jindal-Snape and Miller, 2010). When both self-worth and self-competence are positive, self-esteem is high. However, in cases where individuals demonstrate a deficiency on one or both dimensions, they can develop pseudo or defensive self-esteem (Mruk, 1999). Individuals who demonstrate self-worth but not self-competence may develop avoidance strategies when they are asked to complete challenges (Jindal-Snape and Miller, 2010). Those who have low self-worth (due to trauma, a history of receiving negative feedback and other adverse experiences) but a positive sense of competence may demonstrate anti-social behaviours. If both constructs are deficient, overall self-esteem is likely to be low. The model is demarcated into quadrants and individuals may fall into any one of the quadrants.

SUMMARY

This chapter has emphasised the role of the curriculum in addressing the needs of the whole child. Throughout the chapter guidance has been provided in relation to children's needs including personal and intellectual development and moral, spiritual and cultural development as well as physical and mental health. It has also outlined the implications of the Department for Education's statutory guidance on Relationships Education. Finally, the chapter has also highlighted the importance of supporting children to acquire an understanding of fundamental British values and the purpose of the curriculum in relation to children's development as good citizens.

FURTHER READING

Glazzard, J and Stones, S (2020) *Relationships Education for Primary Schools*. St Albans: Critical Publishing.

Hoyle, A and McGeeney, E (2019) *Great Relationships and Sex Education: 200+ Activities for Educators Working with Young People.* Oxon: Routledge.

+CHAPTER 8

CHARACTER EDUCATION

CHAPTER OBJECTIVES

After reading this chapter you will understand:

+ the aims of character education;

+ the importance of adopting a whole-school approach to character education;

+ the importance of culture, behaviour, resilience and confidence;

+ how to integrate character education into the curriculum;

+ how co-curriculum and volunteering opportunities can contribute to character education;

+ how to promote equality of opportunity within the delivery of character education.

INTRODUCTION

This chapter introduces the concept of character education and emphasises the importance of values, attitudes, skills and behaviours. It also considers the implications of character education within the context of school responsibilities. Additionally, the chapter provides guidance in relation to the key challenges that schools are likely to experience with their planning and delivery of character education. There is some discussion on the importance of character education and this is situated within the requirements of the statutory guidance. The chapter also considers character education in relation to positive school culture and the role of the leadership team is outlined. Some guidance is provided to support schools to develop learners' resilience and confidence and we emphasise the importance of co-curriculum and volunteering opportunities. Finally, the chapter emphasises the role that schools play in promoting equality of opportunity and some guidance is provided to support teachers and school staff.

WHAT IS CHARACTER EDUCATION?

Character education aims to develop a set of values, attitudes, skills and behaviours which support personal development and contribute to positive long-term outcomes (Walker et al, 2017). Character education aims to support children to develop moral and civic values. This enables them to understand the difference between right and wrong and to understand their responsibilities as citizens to the local and global communities in which they live.

There is no correct approach to delivering character education in schools. However, it is important that school leadership teams view the development of character as being central to the culture, values and vision of the school (Walker et al, 2017). It is also important to adopt a whole-school approach (Walker et al, 2017). This ensures that specific character virtues are consistently reinforced in all classrooms. It is also important that teachers and leaders exemplify the character virtues that they want children to develop (Walker et al, 2017). This has implications for the way in which adults speak to children.

Some children live their lives surrounded by adults in their families and in the wider community who do not demonstrate positive character virtues. It is important to be aware that the values that the school seeks to promote may be in direct conflict with the values that are consistently demonstrated in homes and communities. In this case, children may have to re-frame their character traits when they are in the context of the school. Some children will internalise the positive character virtues that the school promotes, and these will shape their identities as they develop. Others will learn to 'switch' on the positive character virtues when they are in school even though they may adopt a different set of virtues when they are outside the school. The key challenge for schools is therefore how to address the dissonance between the character virtues that are promoted outside of school and those that are promoted within school. More significant though is how schools support children to internalise the positive character virtues that are essential to long-term success so that they consistently demonstrate them, believe in them and subsequently reject the negative character virtues that they are exposed to outside of school.

CRITICAL QUESTIONS

+ How might social and cultural contexts influence the development of character?

+ Why do you think that character education has become a policy priority?

THE IMPORTANCE OF CHARACTER

Although character education is not identified as a separate strand within the statutory guidance (DfE, 2019b), it is embedded within specific themes. Within 'caring friendships' specific character traits are addressed. Character traits include respect, motivation, emotional and social regulation, social confidence, social and communication skills, trustworthiness, resilience, leadership, loyalty, kindness, courtesy, truthfulness, courage and generosity. Within 'respectful relationships' courtesy and manners are identified as key character traits. Character education is therefore part of relationships education in primary schools.

The statutory guidance states:

A growing ability to form strong and positive relationships with others depends on the deliberate cultivation of character traits and positive personal attributes, (sometimes referred to as 'virtues') in the individual.

(DfE, 2019a, p 20)

Character is a complex concept and multifaceted. Important aspects include:

+ the ability to stay motivated by long-term goals, including the ability to invest effort and persevere with something despite setbacks;

+ the development of moral attributes or virtues;

+ the acquisition of social confidence, including the ability to make persuasive arguments, listen to others and demonstrate good manners and courtesy toward others;

+ the ability to appreciate the importance of long-term commitments, for example by demonstrating commitment to a relationship, a vocation, a faith or world view or a commitment to the local community.

(DfE, 2019b)

The *Education Inspection Framework* (Ofsted, 2019a) embeds character education within the strand of 'personal development'. Inspectors will evaluate the curriculum and the school's work in supporting learners to develop their character, including their resilience, confidence and independence.

CRITICAL QUESTIONS

+ How can resilience be embedded into the curriculum?

+ How can the curriculum be designed so that it fosters intrinsic motivation?

EVIDENCE-BASED PRACTICE

Evidence suggests that character education supports the development of a positive school culture, leads to a more conducive learning environment and fosters improved behaviour, attendance and motivation (OECD, 2015; Walker et al, 2017). It also leads to positive long-term outcomes including facilitating access to higher education (Walker et al, 2017) and promotes good mental well-being (DfE, 2019b; Taylor et al, 2017). Research suggests that character education drives equality and social mobility (Chanfreau et al, 2016).

DEVELOPING A CURRICULUM THAT FOSTERS MOTIVATION

Motivation is an important character trait because it helps us to achieve goals. Extrinsic motivators can support children in completing tasks. However, the aim of an effective curriculum is to promote intrinsic motivation. Teachers can encourage children to be motivated not by extrinsic rewards but by the curriculum itself. Providing children with a rich and broad curriculum which enables them to undertake deep learning will support children's motivation. Intrinsic motivation can be fostered through:

+ active learning opportunities which enable children to learn through first-hand experiences;

+ planning a curriculum which is contemporary, relevant and related to children's interests;

+ planning a curriculum which allows children to take risks;

+ integrating problem-based learning into the curriculum;

+ providing opportunities for collaborative learning;

+ allowing children to become absorbed in a task rather than moving them too quickly onto the next lesson;

+ changing the context in which learning takes place so that subjects are not always taught within the classroom;

+ making investigation central to curriculum design so that children work, for example, as scientists, historians, archaeologists, geographers and engineers;

+ ensuring that play-based pedagogy is central to early years education.

The curriculum can be used to enhance children's motivation by supporting them to recognise that intelligence can grow and be developed through effort. If children develop a view that intelligence is static, then it is highly likely that they will become demotivated. Motivation is enhanced through achievement and the curriculum plays a crucial role in preparing students to achieve. Children achieve well when they invest effort into their learning and if they demonstrate resilience when they are working on challenging tasks. It is therefore essential that children recognise that the brain is malleable and this is likely to be motivating as this perspective offers a sense of encouragement and hope.

Existing research demonstrates that improving achievement enhances both motivation and confidence. According to Coe et al (2014), it is likely that teachers who are confronted with the poor motivation of low-attaining students will interpret this as the cause of low attainment. In response teachers assume that it is necessary and possible to address motivation before attempting to teach new material. However, evidence demonstrates that these attempts are unlikely to achieve the desired outcome and that in all cases the impact on subsequent learning is close to zero (Coe et al, 2014). Instead, if the curriculum allows children to succeed then increased motivation and confidence should follow.

DEVELOPING SOCIAL AND COMMUNICATION SKILLS THROUGH THE CURRICULUM

Children use verbal and non-verbal communication for a range of purposes. These include showing, exchanging, asking, sharing and commenting. As children develop they learn how conversation works by observing social situations. This supports children to learn how social interaction works which allows them to begin to communicate with others. It is therefore clear that a child's ability to develop conversationally and socially is in part dependent upon opportunities for interaction with others. These opportunities are crucial as the development of communication skills is strongly linked to a child's capacity to express feelings and thoughts as well as make friends and feel understood (DoET Victoria, 2016). Furthermore, a child's ability to interact successfully with others through the management of emotion and behaviour is linked to progress in a range of developmental areas (Mashburn et al, 2008). It is also linked to the emergence of self-identity, well-being and social and academic progress in primary school (Webster-Stratton and Reid, 2004).

Conversation and social skills must be modelled throughout the curriculum. Interactions with children should be used to demonstrate conversation and social skills and children should be encouraged to take part in non-verbal activities including games and turn-taking. Facilitating back-and-forth exchanges can support children to develop their skills of interaction. Opportunities should also be offered within the curriculum to expose children to interaction between adults and peers in order to model conversational discussion and to illustrate what listening and empathy look like.

CASE STUDY

OFFERING OPPORTUNITIES FOR SOCIAL INTERACTION

RECEPTION TO YEAR 6

Within the classroom environment you should set up spaces which encourage interaction between peers and with adults. Within this space it is also valuable to offer opportunities for play, performance and storytelling as well as reading and writing in order to provide opportunities for children to apply their skills to everyday situations. Using engaging materials can be helpful to facilitate shared play and social interaction as can offering game play, which involves elements of sharing, exchange and team work.

PROMOTING RESILIENCE THROUGH THE CURRICULUM

Grit and resilience are important characteristics which influence achievement. Although these terms are sometimes used interchangeably, it is important to recognise that there are some key differences between them. Grit is often associated with sustained perseverance towards long-term goals (Duckworth et al, 2007). On the other hand resilience is usually used to describe overcoming situations of adversity, although this is not uncontroversial (eg, see Roffey, 2017).

Children who demonstrate resilience can recover from adverse situations and this can support them in achieving goals. However, the concept of resilience is problematic because resilience is relational; that is, a person's ability to be resilient is influenced by their relationships with others. Children are more likely to have greater resilience if they have access to social support networks which can offer emotional and practical support during challenging times. Access to supportive teachers, peers, family and community support can enable individuals to be resilient during times when they experience adversity. In addition, resilience is also contextual. Resilience varies from one context to another and it is therefore possible to demonstrate greater resilience in some contexts than it is in others.

SOCIAL AND EMOTIONAL REGULATION SKILLS

Research demonstrates that developing children's social and emotional regulation skills supports positive longer-term outcomes (Goodman et al, 2015) and in the early years Roffey (2017) emphasises the importance of social and emotional learning. Interactions with significant others and the communities in which children live influence social and emotional development. Social learning theory argues that children will replicate the behaviour that they are exposed to. Therefore, it is clear that if children have not been exposed to clear boundaries in the context of their home environment then they may come into an early years setting with the belief that behaviours which are tolerated in the home will be tolerated in the pre-school, nursery or school. Children may display resistance and negative behaviours and will need to be given time to adjust to these new expectations. These social and emotional behaviours may also be an attempt to communicate an unmet need. Practitioners need to be sensitive to the reasons why these behaviours may occur and it is important to remember that children who experience adverse situations in the home or community environment may demonstrate a range of inappropriate behaviours.

DEVELOPING LEADERSHIP SKILLS THROUGH THE CURRICULUM

One of the best ways of empowering children is to develop their leadership skills. Leadership is an important life skill which is useful in education, employment and in social and family contexts.

One way of developing leadership skills is to incorporate collaborative learning into the curriculum. Group projects enable children to work towards a desired goal, organise and manage their workload, monitor their progress, and distribute work across members of a group. These types of projects support the development of planning and evaluation skills. These are metacognitive skills which are essential for future success.

Implicit and explicit opportunities to learn leadership skills can and therefore should permeate the curriculum as well as the culture of the school or setting. This can support children to develop a selection of leadership languages and tools that they will need in later life. These can be taught as discrete and specific behaviours as well as through wider enrichment and extracurricular events, drop down days and cross-curricular activities which provide opportunities for children to explore learning within the context of their own aspirations and needs. These events and activities provide opportunities for children to apply and develop their skills in contextual age-appropriate scenarios and situations.

THE ROLE OF THE CURRICULUM IN PROMOTING MORAL DEVELOPMENT

The curriculum plays an essential role in supporting children to acquire an understanding of the difference between what is right and what is not and of moral conflict as well as being concerned for others and the desire to do what is right. Moral development is crucial for all children and should be incorporated in the curriculum. All subjects within the curriculum provide opportunities to promote moral development. In addition to the curriculum the school ethos also makes a significant contribution to moral development as do whole-school enrichment and extracurricular activities.

One way of promoting moral development within the curriculum is to facilitate opportunities for children to engage in discussion and debate using circle time. Children should be taught to reflect on the principles underpinning the decisions that they make so that decisions are not determined by the sanctions or consequences that follow. Encouraging children to make judgements can support them to take responsibility for their own actions and behaviours. In this way the curriculum should support children to recognise the importance of respecting and helping others, being considerate and exercising self-discipline while developing high expectations of their own behaviour, conduct and decision-making.

PROMOTING COMMITMENT THROUGH THE CURRICULUM

The curriculum should prepare children for the challenges that they will face in their next stage of learning as well as in later life. It is crucial that the curriculum provides experiences for children to engage in and commit to their own learning with the confidence to think independently and take responsibility for their own learning.

Offering students activities and opportunities that they can commit to is one way that the curriculum can be used to promote a sense of commitment. This allows children to reflect on the commitments that they have. If children express an interest in quitting or giving up a commitment, then you should explain why it is important to be resilient and persevere. This modelling and exemplification of commitment can support character development and help children to recognise values and priorities in a beneficial way.

DEVELOPING A POSITIVE SCHOOL CULTURE

School leaders are responsible for creating the school ethos and culture. The school ethos should embody a strong vision for character and personal development (DfE, 2019b). The importance of positive virtues and character traits should be embodied within the vision. These might include resilience, self-regulation, social behaviours and virtues. An effective school leadership team will foster a sense of pride, belonging and identity among all members of the school community.

DEVELOPING POSITIVE BEHAVIOUR

Research suggests that childhood self-control predicts achievement and adjustment outcomes, even in adulthood (Gutman and Schoon, 2013). Good behaviour is an essential characteristic of effective schools. It creates the conditions for effective learning and it prepares children for life after leaving school. Good discipline also ensures that schools are safe places for all members of the school community. An essential aspect of character education is to promote positive social behaviours so that children can learn effectively and are well prepared for adult life.

Children should be taught about the importance of demonstrating respect towards others, regardless of any differences. Demonstrating respect is a fundamental characteristic of an inclusive society. Teaching children about good manners and courtesy ensures that they can conduct themselves appropriately within educational, social and workplace contexts. This is particularly important in cases where children do not live in families or communities where these virtues are demonstrated.

A CURRICULUM WHICH PROMOTES CONFIDENCE

An individual's confidence can vary across social, academic and other domains and it can vary in different contexts. It is also influenced by one's self-worth and self-efficacy. Self-efficacy is an individual's appraisal of their own competences within specific domains, whereas self-worth is an individual's overall view of themselves based on evaluations that others (peers, family, teachers) have made of them. Both self-efficacy and self-worth contribute to overall self-esteem. It is possible for both aspects to be high or low or for one to be high and the other to be low. Overall, self-esteem affects confidence.

The good news is that resilience and confidence are dynamic traits and can be altered. Supportive school environments can buffer against the effects of negative environments within homes and communities which detrimentally impact both resilience and confidence. Children can be taught to develop their resilience, for example, by teaching them to recover from 'failure' or teaching them to be resilient to feedback. Exposure to teachers who empower children can dramatically improve a person's confidence. In addition, the experience of academic success is a vital ingredient for improving confidence. As children begin to realise that they are capable of achieving, their self-efficacy starts to improve and this improves their self-esteem and confidence. Children can be taught to demonstrate social confidence in specific situations, even if they do not feel confident. They can be taught how to appear confident but more importantly a skilled teacher can provide children with genuine confidence by getting them to believe in themselves.

Access to a well-designed curriculum helps children to develop confidence. Knowledge and skills should be sequenced correctly. This enables children to make sense of new subject content because correct sequencing provides them with the foundational knowledge and skills upon which new content can be accommodated. In addition, access to a broad and rich curriculum which provides children with cultural capital is essential for developing social confidence and social mobility. One way of achieving this is to develop their vocabulary and knowledge so that children from all social backgrounds can experience and benefit from the same opportunities.

EVIDENCE-BASED PRACTICE

Research has found that specific character traits are associated with positive outcomes. These are summarised below.

+ *High self-efficacy is associated with better performance and greater persistence and motivation.*

+ *High levels of intrinsic motivation are associated with greater persistence and achievement.*

+ *Good self-regulation, including the ability to delay gratification, is associated with greater attainment.*

+ *High levels of resilience are associated with greater wellbeing.*

+ *Mindsets are malleable and supporting children to develop a growth mindset may result in small to medium size improvements in later performance.*

(Gutman and Schoon, 2013)

Research demonstrates that children who are focused on intrinsic-related goals for engaging in an activity show greater motivation, more persistence and higher achievement compared to children who are focused on extrinsic-related goals (Gutman and Schoon, 2013). Studies have shown that the ability to self-regulate is a significant predictor of attainment (Moffitt et al, 2011). There is also evidence that teaching children to develop appropriate social behaviour improves attainment (Durlak et al, 2011).

DEVELOPING THE CO-CURRICULUM

As part of the character education curriculum, schools should ensure that there is strong provision for co-curricular activities. A well-planned co-curriculum can build social confidence and self-esteem and improve motivation, attendance and academic outcomes for children (DfE, 2019b). Research demonstrates that participation in outdoor adventure programmes has positive effects on the psychological, behavioural, physical and academic outcomes of young people (Gutman and Schoon, 2013).

Activities may include access to sporting or other physical activities, performance, the arts, volunteering, debating, cooking and participation in service. This is not an exhaustive list. The critical point is that schools should ensure that all pupils can participate in the co-curriculum, including those pupils who are the most disadvantaged. Barriers to participation may include the direct costs of activities and to address this schools should subsidise activities to prevent financial constraints becoming a barrier to equal opportunities. The co-curriculum should be designed to enable young people to compete and perform. These opportunities improve social confidence and self-esteem.

DEVELOPING AND PROMOTING THE VALUE OF VOLUNTEERING THROUGH THE CURRICULUM

Volunteering empowers children by enabling them to make a positive contribution to their local community. It helps children to develop a civic mindset and provides them with an opportunity to engage in meaningful work. Children can participate in a range of volunteering opportunities. These may include fundraising activities for local and national organisations, protecting the environment and providing services to elderly people in the local community. Research findings suggest that volunteering produces moderate effects for academic outcomes and small effects for non-cognitive outcomes including social skills, self-perceptions and motivation (Gutman and Schoon, 2013).

CASE STUDY

DEVELOPING RESILIENCE THROUGH THE CURRICULUM

RECEPTION TO YEAR 6

In the classroom environment it is common for practitioners to step in too quickly and offer children a solution to a problem that they may be encountering. However, it is essential to provide children with the time and space that is needed to respond to and deal with challenges. This supports children to experiment with a range of different approaches which promotes key problem-solving skills and develops resilience. While it may be necessary to provide open-ended questions to support children's thinking this should not replace the opportunity for children to problem-solve and experiment.

DEVELOPING EQUALITY OF OPPORTUNITY

School leadership teams need to identify the barriers to participation in relation to some of the activities outlined in this chapter. Barriers could include the cost and timing of activities, lack of parental support and lack of confidence in children. Leadership teams should consider how these barriers will be addressed so that children from all backgrounds have opportunities to participate, particularly in the co-curriculum. The co-curriculum provides children from the most disadvantaged backgrounds with cultural capital by developing a broader range of interests, knowledge and skills. Access to a co-curriculum and volunteering improves social confidence and self-esteem which contribute to social mobility.

SUMMARY

This chapter has emphasised the concept of character education and it has outlined the responsibility of schools in relation to the promotion of values, attitudes, skills and behaviours. It has also considered the implications of character education within the context of school responsibilities and statutory guidance. Guidance has been provided to support schools with the challenges that they may face with the planning and delivery of character education. There has also been some discussion on the importance of character education and we have considered character education in relation to positive school culture and the role of the leadership team. Some case study material has been offered to support your reflection of existing practice and we have encouraged you to consider the benefits of co-curriculum and volunteering. The chapter has also outlined how teachers and school staff can promote equality of opportunity.

FURTHER READING

Rae, T and Wood, J (2019) *The Essential Resilience & Wellbeing Toolkit for Early Years & Younger Children: Activities & Strategies for Professionals & Parents.* Banbury: Hinton House Publishers Ltd.

Smith, G and Pye, S (2018) *Character Education: The Star Awards Programme for Primary Schools.* London: Rising Stars Ltd.

✚ CHAPTER 9

A LANGUAGE- AND ORACY-RICH CURRICULUM

CHAPTER OBJECTIVES

After reading this chapter you will understand:

+ the importance of language within the context of learning and the national curriculum;

+ the requirement for children to learn about the five registers of communication;

+ the importance of drama within the curriculum;

+ key strategies and approaches to support the teaching of drama;

+ how to develop a reading curriculum.

145

INTRODUCTION

This chapter introduces the importance of spoken language and reading and writing within the context of the national curriculum. It emphasises the importance of planning and providing opportunities for children to use spoken language across the entire curriculum, as well as in English, and the benefits of doing so are outlined. The chapter then identifies the five registers of communication and in doing so it outlines the importance of children being taught to understand that they will need to vary their style of communication according to their context. The importance of drama is highlighted in relation to verbal and non-verbal forms of communication and children's writing skills as well as their confidence, self-esteem and collaborative skills. We acknowledge that some teachers may lack confidence with the teaching of drama and strategies and approaches are offered to address this. Finally, the chapter offers guidance and practical strategies to support you to develop a reading curriculum, and we emphasise the importance of children accessing opportunities to develop reading skills throughout and across the curriculum.

THE IMPORTANCE OF LANGUAGE

The national curriculum highlights the importance of spoken language:

The national curriculum for English reflects the importance of spoken language in pupils' development across the whole curriculum – cognitively, socially and linguistically. Spoken language underpins the development of reading and writing.

(DfE, 2013, p 13)

Teachers should plan opportunities for pupils to use spoken language across the curriculum and not just in English. Children should learn to develop the skills of social communication, such as eye contact, active listening and turn-taking. They should use spoken language for discussions, debates, presentations, improvisation and role play, and performances in all subjects of the national curriculum.

Language is critical to literacy development and it supports all-round cognitive development. A child's language skills at the age of two influence strongly their school readiness at the age of five and can influence overall educational outcomes later in childhood. Five year-olds with poor language and literacy development are at greater risk of low educational achievement at the age of seven and beyond.

Good spoken language supports thinking and reasoning skills. Spoken language is therefore crucial to learning across the curriculum. The Communication Trust states:

+ *Spoken language skills underpin literacy development and the development of vocabulary to support reading fluency and comprehension.*

+ *There are strong links between spoken language skills and educational achievement.*

+ *Communication skills help children to develop relationships.*

+ *Many children and young people at risk of underachieving have weaker language skills.*

+ *A focus on spoken language can help to reduce the gap in attainment.*

(The Communication Trust, nd)

Children from poor socio-economic backgrounds tend to have weaker early language skills than those from higher socio-economic backgrounds. Vocabulary is the main indicator of young children's language skills. The vocabulary gap is relatively large for three year-olds from different social backgrounds and this widens when they reach the age of five. On average, children from low socio-economic backgrounds are almost 12 months behind their peers from higher socio-economic backgrounds in vocabulary by the time they start school. Children with delayed language skills from poor backgrounds are less likely to catch up with their peers. In addition, children living in poverty who experience language delay at the age of three are significantly more likely to be behind in literacy at the age of 11 than children from more affluent backgrounds who experience language delay. Also, children from less affluent backgrounds who score well in vocabulary tests at age three are more likely to fall behind their peers from more affluent backgrounds by the age of five. Social disadvantage is associated with higher levels of stress and anxiety among parents which makes it more difficult for them to support their child's early development (Katz et al, 2007). Low-income parents are also less likely to read with their children at home (Malin et al, 2014).

CASE STUDY

DEVELOPING EARLY LANGUAGE SKILLS

EARLY YEARS AND YEAR 1

A school became increasingly concerned about the under-developed language skills of children entering the early years. Teachers and senior leaders were concerned about the number of children who were working below age-related expectations in language and communication at the end of EYFS. Leaders had noticed that children who did not achieve age-related expectations at the end of EYFS also did not achieve age-related expectations in reading and writing at the end of Key Stages 1 and 2.

Various strategies were implemented to address the problem. The school decided to give greater priority to language and communication skills in the early years and in Key Stage 1. Teachers prioritised modelling language and communication skills, including the development of children's vocabulary skills. Play-based pedagogy was prioritised in the early years and adults focused on intervening in children's play to develop their language skills. In Year 1 greater emphasis was given to the use of spoken language in all subjects and communication skills were modelled continuously. The school introduced a series of interventions for pupils who needed development in vocabulary, speaking in sentences and social communication.

The school also planned a series of workshops for parents. These covered a range of aspects including the importance of spoken language in literacy development and ways in which parents could support their child's development in language and communication at home. Parents who did not speak English were provided with a separate course to support the development of their English skills.

REGISTERS FOR EFFECTIVE COMMUNICATION

The national curriculum includes a requirement for children to learn about different registers of communication. There are five registers of communication.

1. *Frozen or static register*: This register rarely or never changes. It can be used when making a pledge or when saying a prayer.
2. *Formal or academic register*: This register includes academic or formal language typically used in speeches or formal announcements.
3. *Consultative register*: This register is formal and typically used in classrooms between teachers and pupils. It is the typical register used within the context of teaching or professional discussions.
4. *Casual register*: This register is used among friends and peers, and includes informal language including slang and colloquialisms.
5. *Intimate register*: This register is usually used between close family members and between people in intimate relationships.

Children essentially need to understand the necessity to vary their style of communication when they are in different contexts. They need to know that the way they communicate with their friends or family is different from the way they should communicate when they are in a formal setting such as a school or when they are talking to someone in a position of authority, such as a teacher. Children need to know that the way they communicate on the playground is different from the way they communicate in a classroom.

SPOKEN LANGUAGE IN THE CURRICULUM

Spoken language is part of the English curriculum. However, it is also an important tool for learning and communication across the curriculum. Teachers should plan for opportunities for children to use spoken language in all subjects through planning activities where children work in pairs or groups. Teachers should also explicitly teach subject-specific vocabulary in different subjects so that children's vocabulary widens.

USING DRAMA IN THE CURRICULUM

Drama is an important pedagogical approach which uses verbal (spoken language) and non-verbal forms of communication. It can support children's understanding in a range of subjects, and it can support the development of children's writing skills. Children can rehearse and use vocabulary in drama which can then be transferred to their writing.

Drama is also useful for developing children's confidence, self-esteem and collaborative skills.

The national curriculum states:

All pupils should be enabled to participate in and gain knowledge, skills and understanding associated with the artistic practice of drama. Pupils should be able to adopt, create and sustain a range of roles, responding appropriately to others in role. They should have opportunities to improvise, devise and script drama for one another and a range of audiences, as well as to rehearse, refine, share and respond thoughtfully to drama and theatre performances.

(DfE, 2013, p 14)

Enrichment, motivation, engagement and the ability to inspire children are sound reasons for doing drama. However, drama can also make a substantial contribution to children's social and emotional development. For some teachers, teaching drama is daunting. They worry that they will lose control of the class. Others worry that the outcomes of the lesson cannot always be predetermined because so much is dependent on children's responses to the drama. One of the reasons why some teachers lack confidence is because they may not know the pedagogical approaches which underpin drama. The following sections outline some of these approaches with the aim of building teachers' confidence. Each strategy can be used across the curriculum and a lesson might focus on providing children experience in a single strategy rather than multiple strategies.

PAIRED IMPROVISATION

Paired improvisation is particularly useful when a decision needs to be made. Imagine that you are reading *Little Red Riding Hood.* Mum asks little Red Riding Hood to take a basket of food to her grandma's house. The children work together in pairs and improvise the conversation. One plays the role of mum and the other child is little Red Riding Hood. The girl does not want to make the journey for numerous reasons (it is too long; too dangerous; too hot; she is too tired). The improvisation is the conversation that takes place between the two people. Mum has to persuade little Red Riding Hood to make the journey through the woods. The children practise the conversation and demonstrate the conversational skills of eye contact, turn-taking and active listening. The children then perform the conversation.

CRITICAL QUESTIONS

+ What skills would the children need to be taught prior to doing paired improvisation?
+ How might you use this strategy in other subjects?
+ How could you use this strategy in Key Stage 2?

TABLEAUX

Children love this strategy. Essentially it is the ability to create a frozen or still image. At first they find it hilarious but you need to encourage them to be serious. They need to be able to hold the image on a given signal until you tell them to stop.

Using the same example of *Little Red Riding Hood* this section explains how to use tableaux. Following the paired improvisation, little Red Riding Hood is about to leave the house to visit her grandma. Ask the children to imagine that they are going to create a still image (or photograph) to depict this scene. What facial expression will little Red Riding Hood have? She might be smiling or crying or she might be angry. What will mum be doing? She might be waving her little girl off. She might be anxious or happy. Ask the children to think about the emotions which can be depicted through non-verbal communication. The children then discuss how to create their frozen image and perfect it. The challenge is for them to hold the image for several seconds when they are given a signal.

CRITICAL QUESTIONS

+ How might you use this strategy in other subjects?
+ How could you use this strategy in Key Stage 2?

THOUGHT TRACKING

Again, we will stick with the same story. Once the children have perfected their tableaux they can be asked to consider what they might be thinking or saying at that specific point in time. It could be a thought, a single word, a caption or a sentence. Red Riding Hood might be fed up about the prospect of having to make the journey through the woods. She might be frightened. She might be excited to see her granny. Mum might be hoping that her daughter will return quickly and safely or she might be relieved to have some time on her own. The children perform the tableaux again. The teacher moves around the room and touches a child on their shoulder. At that point the child must say a word, caption or sentence to express how they are feeling or to demonstrate what they are saying to the other person in the tableaux at that point in time.

CRITICAL QUESTIONS

+ How might you use this strategy in other subjects?

+ How could you use this strategy in Key Stage 2?

HOT SEATING

Little Red Riding Hood meets the Wolf in the woods. She has never seen a wolf before and although she is frightened, she has lots of questions that she wants to ask him. The children work in pairs. One child plays the Wolf and the other is little Red Riding Hood. The children will need time to think of the questions and prepare responses. Little Red Riding Hood decides to ask the following questions: Where do you live? What is your favourite food? Do you have a family? Are you dangerous? Where are you going next? The Wolf is given time to prepare suitable responses to each question. The children then perform the hot seating activity.

CRITICAL QUESTIONS

+ What prior knowledge might children need before they undertake this activity?

+ How might you model this strategy to children?

+ How could you use this strategy in history, science and art to develop children's knowledge of famous people?

+ How might the lesson described here support a subsequent writing activity?

If you are doing hot seating with very young children, you need to be sure that they understand what a question is. You should not assume that children understand the difference between a statement and a question. You will need to explicitly teach children about question words before they undertake an activity like this. One useful strategy for developing their understanding is to provide them with a list of questions and statements and ask the children to sort them into two categories.

CONSCIENCE ALLEY

This strategy is particularly useful in Key Stage 2 but it can also be used in Key Stage 1. The class divides into two lines and they stand face to face with a gap (alley) between them. Each line takes on an opposing point of view. Choose a child to walk through the alley. The child visits each person in the line (usually zigzagging) and each person in the line gives a perspective to represent the point of view that they are adopting. When they reach the end of the alley, the selected child must decide which viewpoint to adopt, having listened to the various perspectives. It allows for the exploration of 'viewpoint' and perspective and can lead into writing discussion/persuasive texts in which there is the need to present two sides of an argument.

In the example of little Red Riding Hood, the children could be asked to perform a conscience alley in response to the question, 'Should little Red Riding Hood visit her grandma's house?'. Two lines would be formed to represent 'yes' and 'no'. Each person standing in the line would be asked to think of a reason to support their stance. One child would be selected to represent little Red Riding Hood. They are asked to walk through the alley and to visit each person. As that person is approached by little Red Riding Hood, they verbalise their reason. When little Red Riding Hood reaches the end of the alley she then decides whether she will visit her grandma.

This activity can be used to support learning across the curriculum in response to different questions which lead to a debate. Consider how it might be used to respond to the following questions.

+ Should animals be kept in zoos?

+ Should children be forced to wear school uniforms?

+ Should a new housing estate be built in the village?

A fantastic story for children in Year 2 or Year 3 is *The True Story of the Three Little Pigs* by Jon Scieszka and Lane Smith. It tells the story but from the perspective of the Wolf. After listening to the story children might be asked to consider whether the Wolf's account is true. Using conscience alley, the children could be asked to consider reasons for why the Wolf is telling the truth or why the Wolf might be lying. Hot seating can also be used to ascertain whether the Wolf is telling the truth by placing the Wolf in the hot seat. The rest of the class can think of questions to ask the Wolf and the Wolf has to respond to each question. At the end of the lesson the children could then be asked to decide whether the Wolf's account is credible.

TEACHER IN ROLE

This activity has been taken from *Enriching Primary English* (Glazzard and Palmer, 2015) to illustrate the strategy of the teacher playing a role.

A teacher has chosen the story of *The Gruffalo* by Julia Donaldson and Axel Scheffler because of the suspense that it creates throughout the text. The children are asked to imagine that they are the Gruffalo. They live in the deep, dark wood and one morning they wake up and decide to go for a walk. After washing in the river the Gruffalo walks further into the forest and stumbles across a house.

The teacher asks :	*Who might live in the house?*
The children respond:	*An old man!*
The teacher asks:	*Why does he live here?*
The children respond:	*He owns the forest!*
The teacher asks:	*Do you think he is lonely?*
The children respond:	*Yes, his family have left him and the animals in the forest are his only friends.*
The teacher asks:	*Shall we talk to him?*
The children respond:	*Yes, but what if he is angry that we have disturbed him?*

They decide to knock on the door. The teacher comes out in role as the old man.

Old man :   *What do you want?*

Children: *We are Gruffaloes and we want to be friends with you.*

At this point the children are 'hooked'. They want this to continue. They want to learn more about the old man. It is at this point that you can divide them into small groups and you can nominate one child per group to be the old man. The rest of the group will then proceed to ask the old man questions so that they can learn more about him. At the same time the old man could think of questions to ask the Gruffaloes. They will need some thinking time in their groups to agree on the questions they want to ask.

The Gruffaloes might want to know:

+ *Why are you on your own?*

+ *What do you do all day?*

+ *How do you get your food?*

+ *What do you eat?*

+ *What is it like living in the forest?*

+ *Which animal is your best friend?*

+ *How did you get to own the forest?*

+ *How do you protect the forest?*

The old man might want to know:

+ *What do Gruffaloes eat?*

+ *What do you do with your sharp teeth?*

+ *What do you do with the purple prickles on your back?*

+ *Why is your tongue black?*

The children are immersed in the drama. They want to continue. However, all of this has developed from the teacher asking the question, *'Who might live in the house?'*. The teacher has used the children's ideas to shape the lesson and the drama is only loosely connected with the original story of *The Gruffalo*. The teacher could not have planned all aspects of the lesson because it was not possible to predict at the planning stage what ideas the children were going to suggest.

The teacher says to the class:

Shall we ask the old man if we can go inside his house to get warm?

After they agree the teacher says:

I wonder what it is like in the old man's house. What might he own?

The teacher gives them time to think this through and provides opportunities for the children to respond with their ideas. The teacher then stops the drama lesson and tells them that they will find out more about the house next week. The teacher leaves them in suspense, looking forward to the next lesson.

A READING CURRICULUM

Reading is a critical life skill and children who leave primary school unable to read are disadvantaged. The emphasis on the teaching of reading changes as children progress in their reading development. Initially, the emphasis is on developing the skill of accurate word recognition through synthetic phonics and whole-word recognition. Language and vocabulary are critical to reading development. Children with more restricted vocabularies are less likely to understand what they are reading, but through reading children can also develop their vocabulary. Once accurate word recognition is secure, greater emphasis can be given to the development of reading comprehension skills. However, both word recognition and linguistic comprehension should be taught concurrently from the early stages of reading development. It is just a question of which skill is given emphasis at different stages of development.

As children develop increasing fluency in reading, they begin to use reading to extend their knowledge. In the early stages of reading development reading is not significantly influenced by intelligence. It is a mechanical skill that children must master. However, as children move from learning to read to reading to learn, reading supports the development of cognition and thus, children's intelligence can be influenced by their ability to read.

It is critical that children develop an enjoyment of reading to support long-term educational and life outcomes. The reading curriculum should therefore promote reading for pleasure. In addition, the texts that teachers choose to use as a basis for curriculum planning should be highly engaging and appeal to children's interests. Teachers who model being readers can powerfully influence children's attitudes towards reading.

There is now a greater emphasis in schools on children reading quality texts. English lessons can be used to discuss characters, settings, plot, structure, vocabulary and the choices that authors make. Children should be supported to evaluate texts and to write their own critical responses. Children should be supported to talk about the books they read with others and to participate in oral debate and discussion in response to what they read. In addition, teachers should consider how to embed reading across the curriculum.

All subjects have specific vocabulary that children should know, understand and use. Subject-specific vocabulary should be visibly on display in lessons and children should have opportunities to read and write across the curriculum. Children who have developed fluency in reading should be encouraged to read to develop their knowledge of subjects. Children should be supported to apply their knowledge of phonics across the curriculum.

It is important however that reading does not become a barrier to learning other subjects in the curriculum. In science emphasis should be given to scientific process rather than on developing children's reading. In history, children who have not developed fluency in reading may struggle to interpret a historical source, which can impact their historical knowledge. In these cases, teachers should identify the barriers to learning and adapt their lessons accordingly so that children are not disadvantaged through the curriculum because of their reading difficulties. In this case, a historical diary extract could be read out, it could be simplified, or an alternative source could be used which does not require reading skills for access. That said, reading is a cross-curricular tool for learning, so opportunities to develop reading skills through the curriculum are important because this provides children with additional practise in reading.

EVIDENCE-BASED PRACTICE

There is increasing evidence which illustrates the importance of reading for pleasure for both educational purposes as well as personal development (Clark and Rumbold, 2006). Research demonstrates that there is a positive relationship between reading frequency, reading enjoyment and attainment (Clark, 2011; Clark and Douglas, 2011).

Reading for pleasure has been reported as more important for children's educational success than their family's socio-economic status (Kirsch et al, 2002). There is consistent evidence that age affects attitudes to reading. Evidence suggests that children enjoy reading less as they get older (Clark and Douglas 2011; Clark and Osborne, 2008; Topping, 2010). However, some evidence suggests that while the frequency with which young people read declines with age, the duration of reading increases with age (Clark, 2011).

Several studies have shown that boys enjoy reading lesser than girls and that children from lower socio-economic backgrounds read less for enjoyment than children from higher socio-economic backgrounds (Clark and Douglas, 2011; Clark and Rumbold, 2006). Having access to cultural capital, such as books and other literacy resources, impacts positively on children's attainment. There is a positive relationship between the number of books in the home and attainment (Clark, 2011). Children who have books of their own enjoy reading for pleasure and read more frequently (Clark and Poulton, 2011).

CASE STUDY

ORAL REHEARSAL

ALL YEAR GROUPS

In one school, children's writing development was below age-related expectations largely because many of the children could not speak in full sentences. School leaders decided to make this a priority in all subjects. A range of approaches supported the development of this skill. These are outlined in the following.

+ Teachers used live modelling to model the process of 'thinking aloud' sentences during the process of whole-class writing composition (shared writing).

+ Children were encouraged to speak in full sentences at every opportunity.

+ During writing tasks children were supported to use the following process:

- *Think it*: pupils think of a sentence to write.
- *Say it*: pupils say the sentence out loud and decide if it makes sense.
- *Count it*: pupils count the number of words in a sentence.
- *Write it*: pupils write the sentence.
- *Read it*: to check for meaning.

+ Children were asked to make sentences from phrases as a key activity in English lessons.

+ Jumbled sentences: children were given a set of words on cards which they had to order to make a complete sentence.

+ Talking boxes: boxes were created in the early years which supported the development of spoken language. Objects of interest were placed in the box which children then talked about. Some of the boxes were 'story boxes' which included a book and puppets to represent characters and scenes. Children used the resources to recreate the story, using spoken language to retell the story.

+ Oral rehearsal in pairs: children were taught to orally communicate their ideas for a writing task to a partner before they started composing their writing. This provided them with an opportunity to orally rehearse their ideas with a partner and to receive peer feedback prior to starting their writing task.

+ Talking frames: children were given structured prompts to support their oral communication in class. These were similar to a writing frame but they supported children through a discussion task so that children knew what to talk about and the structure of the conversation.

EVIDENCE-BASED PRACTICE

The *All Together Now* report was published by the Communication Trust in 2011. The report outlines the importance of communication for children's development and it emphasises the role of communication in relation to children being able to understand and be understood. It also argues that communication is the foundation of relationships as well as being essential for learning, play and social interaction. The report demonstrates how communication impacts all areas of life. In summary, these impacts include:

+ *50 to 90 per cent of children with persistent communication needs subsequently experiencing reading difficulties;*

+ *vocabulary at age 5 being a very strong predictor of the qualifications achieved at both school leaving age and beyond;*

+ *the reading skills of 5 year olds with good and poor oral language skills were considered; when these children were 6, a gap of a few months in reading age had appeared; when these young people reached 14, the gap had widened to a difference of 5 years in reading age;*

+ *only 20 per cent of children with speech, language and communication needs reach the expected levels for their age in English and mathematics by the age of 11, and only 10 per cent achieve 5 good GCSEs (including English and mathematics);*

+ *employers rate communication skills as their highest priority (above qualifications) with 47 per cent of those in England reporting difficulty in finding employees with an appropriate level of oral communication skills;*

+ *more than 80 per cent of long-term unemployed young men have been found to have speech, language and communication needs;*

+ *poor communication being a risk factor for mental health;*

+ *40 per cent of young people aged 7–14 that were referred to child psychiatric services had a language impairment;*

+ *approximately 33 per cent of children with speech, language and communication needs will require treatment for mental health problems in adult life unless further intervention is offered.*

(The Communication Trust, 2011)

SUMMARY

This chapter has emphasised the role of the curriculum in relation to children's spoken language and reading and writing skills. It has provided guidance to support you to plan and provide opportunities for children to develop these skills across the curriculum. In doing so, we have highlighted that these opportunities must extend beyond the teaching of English as a subject discipline. The contribution that drama can make to children's development has been discussed and practical advice has been offered to support teachers to deliver this subject with confidence. The chapter has also outlined the relationship between reading and knowledge and the importance of the reading curriculum so that children can develop these skills across the wider curriculum.

FURTHER READING

Knight, R (2020) *Classroom Talk.* St Albans: Critical Publishing.

Quigley, A (2020) *Closing the Reading Gap.* Oxon: Routledge.

✚ CHAPTER 10
REDESIGNING A
WHOLE-SCHOOL CURRICULUM

CHAPTER OBJECTIVES

After reading this chapter you will understand:

+ the process of designing a whole-school curriculum;

+ how to involve key stakeholders in curriculum design.

INTRODUCTION

Redesigning a whole-school curriculum is a complex task for school leaders. This chapter outlines some approaches for redesigning the curriculum in partnership with key stakeholders. It covers aspects that subject leaders will need to address and it suggests solutions for addressing staff resistance.

Curriculum development is a process that takes time. School leaders are advised to develop a three-year implementation plan so that the process is gradual rather than rapid. It is important to recognise that there will be many positive aspects of the existing curriculum which can be incorporated into the revised curriculum. Changing everything is not necessary and could result in significant additional workload for staff. Changing everything at once is likely to be overwhelming for staff and therefore a gradual process of implementation is preferable.

PRESENTING A RATIONALE FOR CHANGE

Senior leaders need to involve staff from the outset in redesigning the whole-school curriculum. It is important that there is a clear rationale which is articulated to staff which justifies the need for change. Leaders need to explain how the proposed changes to the curriculum will improve outcomes for children. It is important that these outcomes are not just reduced to examination results. The initial consultation with staff should address three key questions.

1. How good is our current curriculum offer?

2. What is working well?

3. What do we need to change?

It is important to recognise that any change is likely to cause anxiety among some staff. They may have been teaching the current curriculum for several years and they may be worried that any changes to the curriculum will lead to additional workload and take them out of their comfort zone. It is important to allow staff to have an opportunity to share their concerns and to offer them reassurance at this point.

The *Education Inspection Framework* (Ofsted, 2019a) has elevated the status of the curriculum in schools. Inspectors are interested in the school's rationale for its curriculum, the knowledge and skills that children are taught and how well these are sequenced to provide children with a coherent learning experience. In previous inspection frameworks there has been a greater focus on outcomes rather than on what children are taught. This has led, in some instances, to children receiving a narrow curriculum and experiencing superficial learning as teachers have focused on teaching to the test. The renewed emphasis on the curriculum in school inspections is important and one of the reasons why school leaders need to review the curriculum. However, this is not the only reason. We live in a society which is rapidly changing. Society is addressing significant social, economic and environmental issues and schools need to make sure that children have the appropriate knowledge and skills to thrive in the twenty-first century. The pace of technological development has been rapid, and schools need to ensure that children can adapt to future developments. A static curriculum does not ensure that children are prepared to address future and current issues. The curriculum must be exciting, dynamic and contemporary so that children are well-positioned to be twenty-first century global citizens. These arguments might support the rationale for change.

Developing a new whole-school curriculum should not result in completely abandoning the current curriculum. There will be many aspects of the current curriculum that are working well and providing children with the right kinds of knowledge, skills and attitudes that will enable them to thrive in the twenty-first century. The starting point in curriculum development is to identify what is working well and therefore what needs to be preserved. Staff will also be able to identify what is not working well, that is, the topics, themes or units of work which they may not enjoy teaching, and which may not be providing children with what they need. Although teachers do have to teach things that they may not like, in general, when teachers enjoy what they are teaching, are passionate and excited about it, they teach well.

The starting point is therefore to open up a discussion about what is working well and what is less effective. However, it must also be acknowledged that the national curriculum already specifies the minimum level of knowledge, skills and attitudes that children need to be taught. Schools cannot therefore ignore this and must view the national curriculum as a minimum curriculum requirement. Schools are free to go beyond the requirements of the national curriculum by designing a curriculum that serves the needs of their pupils and the communities which they serve. In mathematics, English and science, there is clear guidance in the national curriculum about the topics that need to be taught in specific year groups. However, the guidance is less prescriptive in the foundation subjects both in terms of curriculum content and when that content needs to be taught. This provides an opportunity for school leaders and their staff to think about how to sequence the curriculum, when to teach content, how to build on it throughout the key stages and when to revisit content. Much greater attention needs to be given to the sequencing of subject-specific content in the foundation subjects so that children develop a secure understanding of these subjects.

EVIDENCE-BASED PRACTICE

It is highly likely that some staff will resist a leader's decision to review or redesign the curriculum offer. This is problematic because resistance to change can be one of the most difficult barriers to overcome when implementing change. The theorists Kotter and Schlesinger (1979) suggest that there are four reasons why staff may resist change. These are:

1. self-interest;

2. low tolerance for change;

3. making a different assessment of the change that is needed;

4. misunderstanding the change or change rationale.

Crucially, these reasons must be understood if it is to be recognised that staff resistance often has no association with selfishness or hostility. Without this understanding, it can often be too easy to assume that resistance is an act of opposition or defence.

That said, in some cases, staff may resist this change because of their own self-interest. They may fear that their own status or security is being threatened and may have responded in such a way as to protect their own interests over those of the school. In these cases, it is important to demonstrate to staff how the curriculum change may benefit them and the children. This could be in relation to the provision of additional opportunities for both staff and children as well as a positive impact on well-being and morale and a reduction in workload.

Staff may also resist change because they have low change-tolerance. These colleagues may be reluctant to change and prefer the 'status quo'. This may occur because stability is valued or previous attempts to implement change have been unsuccessful. For example, an earlier redesign of the curriculum may have lost momentum despite significant investment in terms of staff time. In these cases, it is important to emphasise that the school is committed to the implementation, monitoring and evaluation of any change as well as the lessons that have been learned from previous change initiatives. It can also be helpful to reflect on the mistakes that might have been made during an earlier programme of change.

Another reason for resistance to change occurs when staff carry out their own appraisal of the situation and this results in an assessment of the change that is different from the one required. For example, a member of staff may feel that a specific approach to curriculum design is more suitable for the context of the school than the approach adopted by leaders. Equally, there may a disagreement in relation to curriculum priorities within the social and cultural context of the school. In these cases, it is essential to probe these alternatives and to understand why staff feel that a different approach may be more appropriate. This supports the 'unpicking' of each, drawing on necessary research, policies and legislation.

Finally, staff may simply resist change because they do not understand why it is required. Alternatively, they may be misinformed following informal dialogue. They may not be aware of changes to statutory guidance and legislation or they may not be aware of the need to respond to changes in the social and cultural context of the school and community. In these cases, education and communication play a crucial role. Staff need to be made aware of why the redesign is required. They should be supported to understand the justification for the change and where necessary any supporting policies and frameworks.

DETERMINING CURRICULUM INTENT

Once staff have a clear understanding about what aspects of the curriculum are working well and what needs to change, it is time for school leaders and staff to consider the intent of the curriculum. The following questions will support this phase of curriculum development.

+ What do we want our learners to know?

+ What skills do we want out learners to possess?

+ What attitudes do we want to instil in our learners?

The process of determining curriculum content will take several weeks. School leaders may wish to develop a series of workshops with stakeholders to discuss these three questions. One way of approaching this is to plan and implement five workshops with each stakeholder group which address these questions. Leaders should consult with staff, pupils, parents and members of the community.

Parents, staff, governors and community members will need to be given some context at the start of the meeting. This might include a discussion about the *Education Inspection Framework*, the rationale for the change and the importance of developing a curriculum which provides children with cultural capital. This is likely to be an unfamiliar term to the stakeholders and it will need to be addressed sensitively with parents, so that they do not feel that their socio-economic background is being undervalued.

The meetings should be genuine consultations which allow stakeholders to discuss the questions in small groups, mind map their responses and share the outcomes of their discussions with the larger group. It is useful to provide large sheets of paper, pens and sticky notes so that there are tangible outputs from the meetings which can then inform curriculum development. These can be reviewed by the senior leadership team to inform curriculum change.

WRITING A STATEMENT OF CURRICULUM INTENT

Following the stakeholder meetings, leaders will need to synthesise the views of staff, governors, pupils and the community into a statement or statements of curriculum intent. There is no mandatory requirement for schools to produce intent statements and such statements are only useful if they are implemented in practice. However, given that inspectors will conduct conversations with leaders about curriculum intent, a statement of policy which articulates curriculum intent is useful, provided it does not become an arduous task.

The statement of curriculum intent should address the following questions.

+ What *knowledge* and *skills* do our learners need to develop and thrive in the twenty-first century?

+ What *attitudes* and *values* does our curriculum promote to enable our learners to thrive as global citizens?

REVIEWING THE EXISTING CURRICULUM

Although the initial discussion addressed the strengths and areas for development of the existing curriculum, it will be necessary for subject leaders to review the curriculum in their subject areas in greater detail. If the school is part of a multi-academy trust (MAT) then subject leaders from across the MAT can work together on reviewing the curriculum with their specific subject(s), particularly if there is an intention to develop a MAT-wide approach to the curriculum.

Subject leaders will need to look carefully at the existing curriculum. This review should address the following aspects.

+ What knowledge and skills do children need to learn?

+ What subject content is a mandatory requirement of the national curriculum?

+ Is the existing curriculum sequenced correctly to ensure that children develop secure subject knowledge and skills?

+ How ambitious is the curriculum?

+ How inclusive is the curriculum?

+ How can cultural capital be embedded in the subject?

+ What training might staff need to implement the revised curriculum?

+ What resources might be needed to implement the new subject curriculum?

IDENTIFYING WHAT NEEDS TO CHANGE

Once subject leaders have completed a curriculum review of the subjects that they lead, they will have started to identify what needs to change. This process can only be completed when there is clear understanding of the intent of the curriculum. Subject leaders can start to identify priorities for curriculum development from the subject leader curriculum review, but it is important that they consider the statement of curriculum intent so that each subject curriculum contributes to the overall agreed statement of intent.

INVOLVING STAKEHOLDERS

Leaders will need to consider how to involve stakeholders in the process of reviewing the curriculum. There are different levels of involvement that leaders could adopt. One level of involvement is to simply inform stakeholders about the changes to the curriculum. However, this model is not inclusive because it does not allow the views of stakeholders to inform curriculum development. A development from this is to provide opportunities for stakeholders to review curriculum plans after they have been developed. The feedback from stakeholders can then inform subsequent curriculum development. A higher level of engagement from stakeholders is to utilise a working group that works together to develop the curriculum. This model is more inclusive because it allows stakeholders to make an active contribution to curriculum development from the start. However, working groups tend not to be effective if they are starting from scratch with a blank sheet of paper. Many of the stakeholders are not experts in the curriculum or even in education. These meetings will be more productive if school leaders take an active role in the meetings by presenting a clear rationale for change and preparing curriculum plans to table at the meetings.

Schools will need to decide how to involve children in the process. It might not be appropriate for children to sit through a lengthy meeting with other key stakeholders. There are other ways of involving children in the process of curriculum review which might be more effective. These include:

+ carrying out focus groups with children from different year groups to ascertain their perspectives on the curriculum;

+ completing a pupil questionnaire to ascertain the children's views on the curriculum;

+ developing a separate working group for children from different year groups to provide an opportunity for them to work on curriculum development with subject leaders.

If consultation with children is taking place separately, school leaders must ensure that the perspectives of the children are discussed at the stakeholder meetings.

THE IMPORTANCE OF SEQUENCING

The *Education Inspection Framework* (Ofsted, 2019a) places a greater emphasis on sequencing than previous frameworks. Subject leaders must ensure that knowledge and skills within their subjects are taught in the correct order so that children's learning is coherent. During the curriculum review of their subject, leaders will need to review the current sequencing of knowledge and skills within and across key stages and within specific units of work. Correct sequencing of knowledge and skills will ensure that children make progress within the subject.

THE IMPORTANCE OF THE SUBJECT

For several years in primary schools, there has been significant attention given to subject-specific knowledge and skills in mathematics, English and science. However, there has been less attention given to subject-specific knowledge and skills in the foundation subjects. This has meant that children have not always developed good subject knowledge across the broader primary curriculum because subject-specific knowledge, concepts and skills have not always been taught or assessed.

In developing a curriculum review in specific subjects, leaders therefore need to identify clearly the subject-specific knowledge and skills that children need to learn to develop secure subject knowledge. Leaders then need to decide when these will be taught and how they will be sequenced.

CASE STUDY

CURRICULUM REVIEW IN ART

ALL YEAR GROUPS

Art subject leaders from across five schools in a multi-academy trust developed a working group to review the curriculum in art and design. They started by reviewing the existing curriculum in art and design. This was complex because each school had developed their own art and design curriculum, but the purpose of the review was to develop a uniform approach to art and design across the MAT.

There was much good practice to share across the schools. Leaders then looked at the subject-specific knowledge, concepts and skills that are essential for pupils to develop good subject knowledge in art and design. They referred to the national curriculum as a starting point. From the national curriculum they identified that colour, pattern, texture, line, shape, form and space were essential dimensions of art that children needed to understand. Children also need to learn about great artists, architects and designers in history. In addition, the national curriculum specifies that developing skills in drawing, painting and sculpture are essential key skills in art and design.

The subject leaders decided to explore painting as a key skill. They discussed the painting skills that children needed to develop in Year 1 and then systematically explored how to build on these in each of the other year groups. They identified that children initially needed to start learning to paint using large brush strokes, progressing to finer brush strokes with increasing control as they moved into Key Stage 2.

Once they had developed a curriculum map for painting, they explored how to build some of the dimensions of art into the skill of painting, for example, colour, pattern, texture, line, shape, form and space. They then examined each of these dimensions separately in more detail. For example, in relation to the dimension of colour they identified that children needed to learn about mixing primary colours and secondary colours, changing primary colours into a secondary colour, how to make colours lighter or darker and how to create effects in colours by adding textures. Subject leaders then discussed what aspects of colour to teach in Year 1, and how to build on this in subsequent year groups within the skill of painting. This process was repeated for the other dimensions of art and design which were linked to the skill of painting.

Subject leaders then discussed drawing and sculpture and for both skills they considered how to teach them in each of the year groups. They mapped the dimensions onto these skills. However, when mapping the dimensions, they had to consider how those dimensions had been addressed within the skill of painting to provide overall coherence.

Teachers then considered the other aspects of art, specifically knowledge of key artists and designers and how to structure this across each of the year groups. This was aligned to other aspects of the curriculum plan, so that when children were being taught painting, the work of significant painters was addressed. When sculpture was being taught, the work of significant sculptors was taught.

The subject leaders decided to identify the skill of printing as a separate skill, although it overlaps with painting. They develop a progression map for teaching printing, which focused on hand and foot printing in Year 1, moving to simple block printing in Year 2 to more complex block printing in Key Stage 2, including lino printing.

Subject leaders considered how to build cultural capital into the art and design curriculum. They built in opportunities for visits to galleries and outdoor museums in each of the different year groups. They also planned for pupils to participate in a community art project in Year 5 and for pupils to work with local artists in all year groups.

The curriculum plans were shared with a working group of key stakeholders who evaluated them and developed them further. Local artists and designers were included on the stakeholder group.

CRITICAL QUESTIONS

+ What are the advantages and disadvantages of a MAT-wide approach to the curriculum?

+ Why is it important to adopt a collaborative approach to curriculum review?

THE ACID TEST OF THE NEW CURRICULUM

Once the 'new' curriculum has been developed, leaders should evaluate it against the following questions:

+ Does the curriculum fulfil the aims of the statement(s) of curriculum intent?

+ How ambitious and challenging is the curriculum?

+ Is the curriculum coherently planned and sequenced?

+ How broad and balanced is the curriculum?

+ How inclusive is the curriculum?

+ Does the curriculum address the minimum requirements of the national curriculum?

CRITICAL QUESTIONS

+ What are the problems with the word 'ambitious' in the context of the curriculum?

+ What problems might arise during the process of developing the intent of the curriculum and how might these be overcome?

CASE STUDY

CURRICULUM REVIEW IN MUSIC

ALL YEAR GROUPS

A model similar to the one outlined in the previous case study was adopted. Music subject leaders worked together to review the music curriculum before passing their proposed plans to a working group of key stakeholders. Local musicians were represented in the stakeholder group.

Leaders used the national curriculum to identify the key elements of music that children need to be taught. These are pitch, duration, dynamics, tempo, timbre, texture, structure and appropriate musical notations. Leaders discussed how to address these elements in each of the year groups. The national curriculum requires that children know about different genres, styles and traditions of music. These were identified and mapped against each of the year groups. The history of music was also aligned to specific units of work in history to provide overall curriculum coherence. Progression in understanding musical notation was also identified and mapped to the year groups.

EVIDENCE-BASED PRACTICE

Research demonstrates that long-term memory is the central structure of human thinking (Clark et al, 2012). Additionally, evidence suggests that we learn new things in the context of what we already know

(Willingham, 2010). Retrieval practice and spaced (or distributed) practice are critical for supporting transfer of information to the long-term memory.

During the process of curriculum review, leaders should build in frequent opportunities to revisit prior subject-specific learning and plan opportunities for retrieval.

CRITICAL QUESTIONS

+ Why might staff resist change?

+ How might senior leaders work with those staff who block change?

A STAGED APPROACH

Rome wasn't built in a day. The curriculum is the most important aspect of a child's education. Changing everything at once might not be feasible or desirable and it might lead to instability in the school. Planning a staged approach to reviewing the curriculum might be more manageable, perhaps by developing two or three subjects each year. This allows the opportunity to learn from practice and to refine future curriculum developments. A sensible approach would be to develop a three-year plan of curriculum development with time built into the plan for reflection and review.

CELEBRATING GOOD PRACTICE

Any change within schools creates instability because staff have become used to specific ways of working. Some staff may initially resist change because they are frightened, worried about additional workload that the changes may create and unconvinced that the planned changes will be successful. It is better to work with those who are enthusiastic. These are the 'change agents' who will support leaders to convince others to adopt the changes. Take every opportunity to celebrate the good practice that is happening in classrooms as a result of the curriculum review. Showcase good work. Use the 'change agents' to convince others. This will help you to push forward with the changes that need to be made.

EVIDENCE-BASED PRACTICE

Force Field Analysis was developed by Kurt Lewin (1951). Lewin identified two forces that exist within organisations: driving forces and restraining forces. When both forces are equal there is a state of equilibrium or status quo. The equilibrium between the forces needs to be altered to bring about change. The theory has direct practical implications for school leaders who are keen to bring about curriculum development. First, it is necessary for leaders to define the change. Second, they need to identify the driving forces and the restraining forces for that change. Leaders then need to create a strategy for strengthening the driving forces, reducing the restraining forces or both. This will help them to successfully implement the desired change.

SUMMARY

This chapter has emphasised the importance of developing a curriculum review in partnership with key stakeholders. It has suggested strategies for collaborating with key stakeholder groups and it has outlined key considerations for subject leaders.

FURTHER READING

Boyle, B and Charles, M (2016) *Curriculum Development: A Guide for Educators.* London: Sage.

Kidd, D (2020) *A Curriculum of Hope: As Rich in Humanity as in Knowledge.* Carmarthen: Independent Thinking Press.

✚ CONCLUSION

This book has emphasised the importance of a broad and balanced curriculum. It has outlined various approaches to curriculum design but has emphasised the importance of teaching subject-specific knowledge, concepts and skills in the right order so that children develop a secure understanding of each subject. It has emphasised the need for children to know the different disciplines which underpin specific subjects so that they are not disadvantaged when they start secondary school. It has highlighted the importance of a curriculum which embeds enquiry as a central pedagogical approach. Children need to learn through rich first-hand experiences. They need opportunities to work as artists, scientists, historians and authors. Although reading, writing and mathematics can be integrated through the curriculum in addition to being taught discretely, it is crucial that subject learning is not diluted. Teachers need clarity on what subject they are teaching and what they want pupils to learn in a lesson. Pupils also need to know what subject they are learning, and they need to understand how one lesson connects to a previous lesson and to a subsequent lesson.

The book has explored what is meant by cultural capital in relation to the primary curriculum. It has argued that providing children with cultural capital allows, to some extent, for schools to compensate for social disadvantage. Children from higher socio-economic backgrounds are advantaged not only in relation to their language skills, but also in relation to their experiences and knowledge. These factors provide them with a cognitive advantage. This book has emphasised the link between cultural capital and social mobility and argued that all children, irrespective of social background or other circumstances, have a right to the same opportunities. We have provided some practical ideas for developing cultural capital, but these are merely intended to be a starting point for your thinking. We have emphasised the importance of developing children's knowledge, skills and vocabularies through the curriculum, thus making the curriculum an important tool for social mobility.

This book has provided comprehensive guidance on how schools can develop a curriculum which is sensitive to the school context, creative, child-centred and which supports children's personal development. We have identified important components of a mental health curriculum and provided school leaders with guidance which will support them in redesigning the curriculum.

Ultimately schools still must teach the national curriculum but this is a minimum requirement. However, schools have autonomy in relation to curriculum design and the experiences they provide pupils with through the curriculum. The curriculum should empower children. It should enable them to address the challenges of the twenty-first century and it should foster the development of inclusive values and attitudes. It should create a more equitable and sustainable society. The curriculum cannot and should not do everything and one size will not fit all. It will need to be adapted for some children and there are others who will require a highly personalised curriculum. The curriculum should be sufficiently flexible to meet the diverse needs of children. Finally, it should create excitement and enjoyment. It should ignite a passion for learning so that pupils remain motivated and engaged.

✚ REFERENCES

Alexander, R, Rose, A and Woodhead, C (1992)
*Curriculum Organisation and Classroom Practice in Primary Schools:
A Discussion Paper. London*: DES.

Barnes, J and Scoffham, S (2017)
The Humanities in English Primary Schools: Struggling to Survive. *Education*,
45(3): 3–13.

**Baumert, J, Kunter, M, Blum, W, Brunner, M, Voss, T, Jordan, A
and Tsai, Y M (2010)**
Teachers' Mathematical Knowledge, Cognitive Activation in the Classroom, and
Student Progress. *American Educational Research Journal*, 47(1): 133–80.

Berliner, D (2011)
Rational Responses to High Stakes Testing: The Case of Curriculum Narrowing
and the Harm That Follows. *Cambridge Journal of Education*, 41(3): 287–302.

Bernstein, B (1971)
Class, Codes and Control. London: Routledge and Kegan Paul.

Boss, A (2007)
Curriculum. New York, NY: Routledge.

**Chanfreau, J, Tanner, E, Callanan, M, Laing, K, Skipp, A and
Todd, L (2016)**
Out of School Activities during Primary School and KS2 Attainment. Centre for
Longitudinal Studies, Working Paper 2016/1. London: Institute of Education,
University College London.

Clark, C (2011)
*Setting the Baseline: The National Literacy Trust's First Annual Survey into
Reading – 2010*. London: National Literacy Trust.

Clark, C and Douglas, J (2011)
*Young Peoples Reading and Writing: An In-Depth Study Focusing on Enjoyment,
Behaviour, Attitudes and Attainment*. London: National Literacy Trust.

Clark, C and Osborne, S (2008)
How Does Age Relate to Pupils' Perceptions of Themselves as Readers?
London: The National Literacy Trust.

Clark, C and Poulton, L (2011)
Book Ownership and Its Relation to Reading Enjoyment, Attitudes, Behaviour and Attainment. London: National Literacy Trust.

Clark, C and Rumbold, K (2006)
Reading for Pleasure: A Research Overview. London: National Literacy Trust.

Clark, R E, Kirschner, P A and Sweller, J (2012)
Putting Students on the Path to Learning: The Case for Fully Guided Instruction. *American Educator*, 36(1): 6–11.

Clotfelter, C, Ladd, H and Vigdor, J (2010)
Teacher Credentials and Student Achievement in High School: A Cross-Subject Analysis with Student Fixed Effects. *The Journal of Human Resources*, 45(3): 655–81.

Coe, R, Aloisi, C, Higgins, S and Major, L (2014)
What Makes Great Teaching? Review of the Underpinning Research? [online] Available at: www.suttontrust.com/wp-content/uploads/2014/10/What-Makes-Great-Teaching-REPORT.pdf (accessed 17 July 2020).

Collado, S, Corraliza, J, Staats, H and Ruiz, M (2015)
Effect of Frequency and Mode of Contact with Nature on Children's Self-Reported Ecological Behaviors. *Journal of Environmental Psychology*, 41: 65–73.

The Communication Trust (2011)
All Together Now. London: The Communication Trust.

The Communication Trust (nd)
Communicating the Curriculum. London: The Communication Trust.

Cooley, C H (1902)
Human Nature and the Social Order. New York, NY: Charles Scribner's Sons.

Coopersmith, S (1967)
The Antecedents of Self-Esteem. San Francisco, CA: Freeman.

Coulby, D (1989)
The Education Reform Act – Competition and Control. London: Cassell Education Limited.

Craft, A (2000)
Creativity Across the Primary Curriculum. Routledge: London.

Darling-Hammond, L (2000)
Teacher Quality and Student Achievement: A Review of State Policy Evidence. *Education Policy Analysis Archives,* 8(1): 1–44.

Department for Education (DfE) (2013)
The National Curriculum in England Key Stages 1 and 2 Framework Document. London: DfE.

Department for Education (DfE) (2015)
Citizenship Programmes of Study: Key Stages 1 and 2. London: DfE.

Department for Education (DfE) (2019a)
Relationships Education, Relationships and Sex Education (RSE) and Health Education: Statutory Guidance for Governing Bodies, Proprietors, Head Teachers, Principals, Senior Leadership Teams, Teachers. London: DfE.

Department for Education (DfE) (2019b)
Character Education: Framework Guidance. London: DfE.

Department of Education and Science (DES) (1992)
Curriculum Organisation and Classroom Practice in Primary Schools. London: DES.

Department of Education and Training Victoria (DoET Victoria) (2016)
Victorian Early Years Learning and Development Framework (VEYLDF). Melbourne: DoET.

Duckworth, A, Peterson, C, Matthews, M and Kelly, D (2007)
Grit: Perseverance and Passion for Long-Term Goals. *Journal of Personality and Social Psychology,* 92(6): 1087–101.

Durlak, J A, Weissberg, R P, Dymnicki, A B, Taylor, R D and Schellinger, K B (2011)
The Impact of Enhancing Students Social and Emotional Learning: A Meta-analysis of School-Based Universal Interventions. *Child Development,* 82: 405–32.

Ehren, M, Gustafsson J, Altrichter, H, Skedsmo, G, Kemethofer, D and Huber, S (2015)
Comparing Effects and Side Effects of Different School Inspection Systems across Europe. *Comparative Education*, 51(3): 375–400.

Fernald, A, Marchman, V A and Weisleder, A (2013)
SES Differences in Language Processing Skill and Vocabulary Are Evident at 18 Months. *Developmental Science*, 16(2): 234–48.

Gayton, S and Lovell, G (2012)
Resilience in Ambulance Service Paramedics and Its Relationships with Well-Being and General Health. *Traumatology*, 18(1): 58–64.

Girls Education Challenge (GEC) (2018)
Thematic Review: Extra- and Co-curricular Interventions. London: GEC.

Glazzard J and Palmer J (2015)
Enriching Primary English. St Albans: Critical Publishing.

Gonzales, N, Moll, L and Amanti, C (2005)
Funds of Knowledge. Mahwah, NJ: Lawrence Erlbaum.

Goodman, A, Joshi, H, Nasim, B and Tyler, C (2015)
Social and Emotional Skills in Childhood and Their Long-Term Effects on Adult Life: A Review for the Early Intervention Foundation. London: Institute of Education/UCL.

Gutman, L M and Schoon, I (2013)
The Impact of Non-cognitive Skills on Outcomes for Young People: Literature Review. London: National Foundation for Educational Research and Cabinet Office.

Jindal-Snape, D and Miller, D J (2010)
Understanding Transitions through Self-Esteem and Resilience. In Jindal-Snape, D (ed), *Educational Transitions: Moving Stories from Around the World* (pp 10–32). London: Routledge.

Jones, K, Tymms, P, Kemethofer, D, O'Hara, J, McNamara, G, Huber, S, Myrberg, E, Skedsmo, G and Greger, D (2017)
The Unintended Consequences of School Inspection: The Prevalence of Inspection Side-Effects in Austria, the Czech Republic, England, Ireland, the Netherlands, Sweden, and Switzerland. *Oxford Review of Education*, 43(6): 805–22.

Katz, I, Corlyon, J, La Placa, V and Hunter, S (2007)
The Relationship between Parenting and Poverty. York: Joseph Rowntree Foundation.

Kirsch, I, De Jong, J, LaFontaine, D, McQueen, J, Mendelovits, J and Monseur, C (2002)
Reading for Change Performance and Engagement across Countries: Results from PISA 2000. Paris: OECD.

Kotter, J P and Schlesinger, L A (1979)
Choosing Strategies for Change. Harvard Business Review, March–April.

Lewin, K (1951)
Field Theory in Social Science. New York, NY: Harper and Row.

Li, D, Deal, B, Zhou, X, Slavenas, M and Sullivan, W (2018)
Moving Beyond the Neighborhood: Daily Exposure to Nature and Adolescents' Mood. Landscape and Urban Planning, 173: 33–43.

Luthar, S (2006)
Resilience in Development: A Synthesis of Research across Five Decades. In Cicchetti, D and Cohen, D J (eds) Development Psychopathology. Risk, Disorder and Adaptation (pp 739–95). Hoboken, NJ: Wiley.

Malin, J, Cabrera, N and Rowe, M (2014)
Low-Income Minority Mothers and Fathers Reading and Children's Interest: Longitudinal Contributions to Children's Receptive Vocabulary Skills. Early Childhood Research Quarterly, 29(4): 425–32.

Martinez, A, Coker, C, McMahon, S D, Cohen, J and Thapa, A (2016)
Involvement in Extracurricular Activities: Identifying Differences in Perceptions of School Climate. The Educational and Developmental Psychologist, 33(1): 70–84.

Mashburn, A J, Pianta, R C, Hamre, B K, Downer, J T, Barbarin, O A, Bryant, D and Burchinal, M (2008)
Measures of Classroom Quality in Prekindergarten and Children's Development of Academic, Language, and Social Skills. Child Development, 79(3): 732–49.

Masten, A and Garmezy, N (1985)

Risk, Vulnerability, and Protective Factors in Developmental Psychopathology. In Lahey, B B and Kazdin, A E (eds) *Advances in Clinical Child Psychology* (pp 1–52). New York, NY: Plenum Press.

Moffitt, T E, Arseneault, L, Belsky, D, Dickson, N, Hancox, R J, Harrington, H and Caspi, A (2011)

A Gradient of Childhood Self-Control Predicts Health, Wealth, and Public Safety. *Proceedings of the National Academy of Sciences*, 108(7): 2693–8.

Montacute, R and Cullinane, C (2018)

Parent Power 2018: How Parents Use Financial and Cultural Resources to Boost Their Childrens Chances of Success. London: The Sutton Trust.

Mruk, C (1999)

Self-Esteem: Research, Theory and Practice. London: Free Association Books.

OECD (2015)

Skills for Social Progress: The Power of Social and Emotional Skills. OECD Skills Studies. France: OECD Publishing.

Office for Standards in Education (Ofsted) (2019a)

Education Inspection Framework. Manchester: Ofsted.

Office for Standards in Education (Ofsted) (2019b)

Inspecting the Curriculum: Revising Inspection Methodology to Support the Education Inspection Framework. Manchester: Ofsted.

Office for Standards in Education (Ofsted) (2019c)

Education Inspection Framework: Overview of Research. Manchester: Ofsted.

Piaget, J (1936)

Origins of Intelligence in the Child. London: Routledge & Kegan Paul.

Reyes, A T, Andrusyszyn, M A, Iwaaiw, C, Forchuk, C and Babenko-Mould, Y (2015)

Resilience in Nursing Education: An Integrative Review. *Journal of Nursing Education*, 54(8): 438–44.

Richardson, M, Sheffield, D, Harvey, C and Petronzi, D (2015)

The Impact of Children's Connection to Nature: A Report for the Royal Society for the Protection of Birds (RSPB). Derby: University of Derby.

Roffey, S (2017)

Ordinary Magic Needs Ordinary Magicians: The Power and Practice of Positive Relationships for Building Youth Resilience and Wellbeing. *Kognition & Pædagogik*, 103: 38–57.

Rogers, C R (1961)

On Becoming a Person. Boston, MA: Houghton Mifflin.

Rose, J (2008)

Independent Review of the Primary Curriculum: Final Report. Nottingham: DCSF Publications.

Sanderson, B and Brewer, M (2017)

What Do We Know about Student Resilience in Health Professional Education? A Scoping Review of the Literature. *Nurse Education Today*, 58: 65–71.

Stallman, H M (2011)

Embedding Resilience within the Tertiary Curriculum: A Feasibility Study. *Higher Education Research and Development*, 30(2): 121–33.

Stephens, D (2013)

Teaching Professional Sexual Ethics across the Seminary Curriculum. *Religious Education*, 108(2): 193–209.

Tafarodi, R W and Milne, A B (2002)

Decomposing Global Self-Esteem. *Journal of Personality*, 70: 443–83.

Tafarodi, R W and Swann, W B (1995)

Self-Liking and Self-Competence as Dimensions of Global Self-Esteem: Initial Validation of a Measure. *Journal of Personality Assessment*, 65: 322–42.

Taylor, R D, Oberle, E, Durlak, J A and Weissberg, R P (2017)

Promoting Positive Youth Development through School-Based Social and Emotional Learning Interventions: A Meta-analysis of Follow-Up Effects. *Child Development*, 88(4): 1156–71.

Thomson, P (2002)

Schooling the Rustbelt Kids: Making the Difference in Changing Times. Unwin: Trentham Books.

Topping, K J (2010)

What Kids Are Reading: The Book-Reading Habits of Students in British Schools, 2010. London: Renaissance Learning UK.

Unicef (1989)
The United Nations Convention on the Rights of the Child. London: Unicef.

Vygotsky, L S (1978)
Mind in Society: The Development of Higher Psychological Processes. Cambridge, MA: Harvard University Press.

Walker, M, Sims, D and Kettlewell, K (2017)
Case Study Report: Leading Character Education in Schools. Slough: National Foundation for Educational Research.

Ward, J, Duncan, J S, Jarden, A and Stewart, T (2016)
The Impact of Children's Exposure to Greenspace on Physical Activity, Cognitive Development, Emotional Wellbeing, and Ability to Appraise Risk. *Health and Place*, 40: 44–50

Webster-Stratton, C and Reid, M J (2004)
Strengthening Social and Emotional Competence in Young Children: The Foundation for Early School Readiness and Success. *Infants & Young Children*, 17(2): 96–113.

White, J (2004)
Rethinking the School Curriculum: Values, Aims and Purposes. London: Routledge.

Willingham, D T (2010)
Why Don't Students Like School?: A Cognitive Scientist Answers Questions about How the Mind Works and What It Means for the Classroom. San Fransisco, CA: Jossey Bass.

Zosh, J M, Hopkins, E J, Jensen, H, Liu, C, Neale, D, Hirsh-Pasek, K, Solis, S L and Whitebread, D (2017)
Learning through Play: A Review of the Evidence (White Paper). Billund, DK: The LEGO Foundation.

+ INDEX